Jesus Did It for You

RECEIVING YOUR INHERITANCE

GREG TEXADA

WESTBOW
PRESS
A DIVISION OF THOMAS NELSON

Unless otherwise indicated, all scripture quotations are taken from the King James Version of the Bible. Scripture quotations marked (AMP) are taken from the Amplified® Bible, Copyright © 1954, 1958, 1962, 1964, 1965, 1987 by The Lockman Foundation. Used by permission. Scripture quotations marked (NLT) are taken from the Holy Bible, New Living Translation, copyright © 1996, 2004, 2007 by Tyndale House Foundation. Used by permission of Tyndale House Publishers, Inc., Carol Stream, Illinois 60188. All rights reserved. Scripture quotations marked (NCV) are taken from The Holy Bible, New Century Version, copyright © 1987, 1988, 1991 by Word Publishing, Nashville, Tennessee. Used by permission.

WestBow Press books may be ordered through booksellers or by contacting:

WestBow Press
A Division of Thomas Nelson
1663 Liberty Drive
Bloomington, IN 47403
www.westbowpress.com
1-(866) 928-1240

Because of the dynamic nature of the Internet, any web addresses or links contained in this book may have changed since publication and may no longer be valid. The views expressed in this work are solely those of the author and do not necessarily reflect the views of the publisher, and the publisher hereby disclaims any responsibility for them.

Any people depicted in stock imagery provided by Thinkstock are models, and such images are being used for illustrative purposes only.

Certain stock imagery © Thinkstock.

ISBN: 978-1-4497-5665-9 (hc)
ISBN: 978-1-4497-5666-6 (sc)
ISBN: 978-1-4497-5667-3 (e)

Library of Congress Control Number: 2012911040

Printed in the United States of America

WestBow Press rev. date: 10/01/2012

Contact Information
Greg Texada
P. O. Box 13195
Alexandria, LA 71303
(318) 442-8100

Contents

Acknowledgment

I give my highest praise and thanks to my Lord Jesus Christ, who has given me purpose and a reason to live. I am amazed by His marvelous grace, patience, and tender mercy. This year I celebrated my 30th birthday as a born again Christian. On the day of my salvation, Satan told me that I would not last two weeks as a Christian. I am glad I did not believe his lies. Jesus, thanks for finding me on March 14, 1982, in a dormitory room at Southern University in Baton Rouge, La. You gave me life that day, and I am forever grateful. Thanks for all the things you did for me and continue to do. Thanks for the love and power you have shown me over the years. I look forward to eternity with you. You still have my heart.

I also want to thank my beautiful wife and sweetheart of 28 years, Celeste. Thanks for believing in me and trusting me with your heart. Thank you for the constant encouragement you have given me and for standing with me in the most difficult times of my life. You are more "Precious" to me today than the day I said, "I do" at the altar. Celeste, I love and appreciate you. I am looking forward to many more years of fruitful service together! We fight till we win!

I also thank God for blessing me with two incredible children, Gabriel and Treasure. They have handled the journey of faith well. Both of you will do extraordinary things with the Lord. Continue to pursue your dreams, and remember that with God, all things are possible.

Everything Jesus did, He did for you, for your benefit. He is alive and seated at the right hand of God in heaven, having secured for you eternal redemption from sin and an inheritance of lifetime blessings now and forever.

CHAPTER 1

— ❧ —

Jesus Did It For You!

For God so loved the world, that he gave his only begotten Son, that whosoever believeth in him should not perish, but have everlasting life. For God sent not his Son into the world to condemn the world; but that the world through him might be saved.

John 3:16-17

This Scripture is a revelation of God's love, grace, wisdom, and power. It demonstrates His desire to save everyone from eternal damnation and give everlasting life to anyone who will believe the good news about Jesus Christ. God loves you so much that He gave Jesus Christ so you would not perish (be lost, ruined, or destroyed) but have everlasting life. This is the gospel in a nutshell.

The Apostle Paul said, "For I am not ashamed of the gospel of Christ: for it is the power of God unto salvation to everyone that believeth" (Romans 1:16). He also stated that the preaching of the cross is foolishness to those who are lost, but to those who are saved it is the power of God. Jesus laid down His life and died for you when He went to the cross. He was buried in a tomb that was heavily guarded by Roman soldiers, but on the third day, God raised Him from the dead. Jesus Christ is alive! He is not dead. He rose again with all authority, dominion, and power in His hands. He is the only Potentate (supreme ruler). He is the King of Kings and Lord of Lords. He is Alpha and Omega, the beginning and the ending, the first and the last, which is, and which was, and which is to the come, the Almighty.

And when I saw him [Jesus], *I fell at his feet as dead. And he laid his right hand upon me, saying unto me, Fear not; I am the first and the last: I am he that liveth, and was dead; and, behold, I am alive for evermore, Amen; and have the keys of hell and of death.*

Revelation 1:17-18

Many people live and die and never understand the significance of His life. They never experience the full benefit of what Jesus did for them when He gave His life on the cross. What happened to Jesus when He went to the cross? What did He experience? Why was the cross necessary? What did He obtain for you by dying? It is more than meets the natural eye. So few ever take advantage of and walk in the blessings that have been provided for them through the death, burial, and resurrection of Jesus Christ.

Blessed be the God and Father of our Lord Jesus Christ, who hath blessed us with all spiritual blessings in heavenly places in Christ:

Ephesians 1:3

God sent Jesus Christ to obtain your salvation so He could bless you with every heavenly blessing. Everything Jesus did, He did for you, for your benefit. He is alive and seated at the right hand of God in heaven, having secured for you eternal redemption from sin and an inheritance of lifetime and eternal blessings.

To open their eyes, and to turn them from darkness to light, and from the power of Satan unto God, that they may receive forgiveness of sins, and inheritance among them which are sanctified by faith that is in me [Jesus].

Acts 26:18

Are you enjoying the inheritance of blessings that Jesus has provided for you? Do you know there is an inheritance with your name on it? It is imperative that you know and understand what Jesus did for you. It is equally essential that you know how to receive (by faith) the blessings and benefits He has provided and made available for you. This revelation (knowing what's yours and how to receive it) is required in order to experience the entire blessing of the Lord. Share the revelation with your children, and tell the good news to everyone.

There are many marvelous blessings and benefits that are now yours as a result of what Jesus Christ did for you. They are all a part of God's plan to bless you and allow you to have heaven on earth. He is ready to reveal Himself to you in a fresh, new light. You will see His glory as He shines His light in your heart and opens your understanding further. You will gain a deeper appreciation for the price Jesus paid for your redemption on the cross. You will learn some key principles on how to receive and enjoy what God has provided for you. Embrace the truths that follow with your whole heart. May the Spirit of wisdom and revelation in the knowledge of Christ rest upon you.

For this cause also thank we God without ceasing, because, when ye received the word of God which ye heard of us, ye received it not as the word of men, but as it is in truth, the word of God, which effectually worketh also in you that believe.

1 Thessalonians 2:13

Make it your great quest in life to stay full of love, exercise patience, and live by faith. Then, watch God do great and mighty things in your life.

Failure to walk in these godly virtues will stunt your growth, neutralize your power, and give Satan an advantage over you that he should not have.

CHAPTER 2

Love ~ Patience ~ Faith

Walking in love, letting patience work, and living by faith are essential to experiencing the full blessing of the Lord in your life. Together, they form a threefold cord that can't be broken. Each is dependent on the other. Faith will not work at its highest level if you don't walk in love because faith is energized by love and compassion. By the same token, it takes faith and trust in God to love others unconditionally. Patience gives love and faith the endurance and perseverance needed to stand strong in adversity until the promises of God become a reality in your life. Love, patience, and faith work together and play a key role in developing godly character and receiving God's best.

Love

A new commandment I give unto you, that ye love one another; as I have loved you, that ye also love one another.

John 13:3-4

And this hope will not lead to disappointment. For we know how dearly God loves us, because he has given us the Holy Spirit to fill our hearts with his love.

Romans 5:5 (NLT)

That Christ may dwell in your hearts by faith; that ye, being rooted and grounded in love, May be able to comprehend with all saints what is the breadth, and length, and depth, and height; And to know the love of Christ, which passeth knowledge, that ye might be filled with all the fulness of God.

Ephesians 3:17-19

You can walk in the same love, compassion, and power that Jesus walked in because when you surrendered your life to the Lord, the love of God was poured into your heart by the Holy Spirit. You now have the ability to love God with all your heart, mind, soul, and strength and to love others unconditionally. Loving others is not a recommendation or suggestion. It is a commandment.

Love is the strength and essence of God's character and nature. Love is the first fruit of the Spirit mentioned in Galatians 5:22. It should be one of the greatest attributes of your life. Jesus said the world would know you are His disciple by the love you give to others. God's desire is that you would become rooted and grounded in love. Every step away from love is a step into darkness and sin.

Walking in the love of God is walking in the light of God's Word. This is demonstrated by caring, sharing, and serving others. Walking in love provides protection and power for living a life that honors God. It protects you from the deceitful strategies and schemes of Satan to fill you with fear, anger, envy, jealousy, or strife. He wants you to be easily offended, to hold grudges against those who have sinned against you, and to have an unforgiving heart. When you do, the flow of God's blessings slows, and your life becomes miserable.

How do you know when you are walking in love? The thirteenth chapter of 1 Corinthians is called the love chapter of the Bible. It reveals the qualities and attributes of the love of God. The love of God endures long and is patient and kind. It is never envious or jealous of others. It is not conceited, arrogant, boastful, haughty, or puffed up with pride. There is a quality of humility and humbleness of mind in the love of God. It is not rude, mean-spirited, or condescending to others. It is not selfish, self-centered, or self-seeking. Love doesn't insist on having its own way. It is not easily offended, touchy, or resentful. It does not keep a record of the evil done to it. It does not rejoice at injustice and unrighteousness. It rejoices when right and truth prevail. Love is ready to believe the best about every person and will not fade way or lose hope under any circumstance. The love of God is strong and will not weaken over time and will never become obsolete. The love of God never fails—and this love is in you.

When walking in love, you will not intentionally mistreat or hurt others. If everyone walked in the love of God, there would be no stealing, killing, lying, jealousy, strife, back-stabbing, or abuse of any kind. There would be no unresolved conflicts, cutting words, broken homes, abandoned children, adulterous relationships, or broken hearts. These things and many more like them are the result of the absence of the love of God. Many are afraid to walk in love because they think they will be taken advantage of or will appear weak. However, there is nothing weak about walking in the love of God. It takes a real commitment.

Walking in love is more than just telling others that you love them. The old saying, actions speak louder than words, is true. Love others with more than just words. Love is an action demonstrating care and service to others. Show others how much you love them by serving them, praying for them, and meeting their needs as led by the Lord. Walking in love keeps you from developing a callous, compassionless heart. It will prevent you from taking advantage of others or taking vengeance upon those who have wronged you. Love provides the power to be a blessing by serving others unselfishly. When you walk in love, God is walking in you—for God is love. Make loving others your great quest in life and your motive for doing what you do. Practice the love of God until you are rooted and grounded in it. Keep yourself in the love of God.

Confession: Father, In the name of the Lord Jesus Christ, I thank you that you have loved me with an everlasting, unconditional love. Nothing can separate me from the love of Jesus Christ. Thank you for working in my life and perfecting those things that concern me. You are working all things together for my good. Your love has been poured forth into my heart by the Holy Spirit, and I am a partaker of your divine nature. You have not given me a spirit of fear, but of power, love, and a sound mind.

I commit to walk in the love of God. I will not walk in unforgiveness, strife, or bitterness. I will not hold grudges or be judgmental or critical towards any person. I will not purposely say or do anything to cause the hurt of another. I will not participate in, rejoice in, or take pleasure in sin and ungodliness. I will not rejoice in the mistakes, failures, or misfortune of others. I will not rehearse or take account of any evil done to me. I have God's love, mercy, and compassion in me. I will keep myself in the love of God.

I commit to tell others of God's love and mercy. I will speak the truth in love. I will look for opportunities to bless, to encourage, and to strengthen others. I will be kind, tenderhearted, and forgiving. I will love God with all my heart, mind, soul, and strength, and I will love others as Christ has loved me.

Patience

> *Knowing this, that the trying of your faith worketh patience but let patience have her perfect work, that ye may be perfect and entire, wanting nothing.*
>
> James 1:3

> *. . . . Cast not away therefore your confidence, which hath great recompence of reward. For ye have need of patience, that, after ye have done the will of God, ye might receive the promise.*
>
> Hebrews 10:35-36

Patience is the quality of being constant, steady, enduring and persevering when things are not going your way. Patience undergirds love and faith and gives the stamina and perseverance needed to endure hardships and stand strong in adversity until the promises are manifested in your life. Patience is a quality that can only be developed through trials, tribulation, and testing of your faith. When you ask God for more patience, get ready for more trouble.

Many have put patience in the unemployment line. When things don't happen as quickly as they think, the first thing they do is fire patience. They give up on God and surrender to contradictory circumstances, doubts, fears, and the trials of faith. Patience is a fruit of the Spirit and is looking for a place to work in your life. Hire patience and let it go to work for you. Patience, coupled with love and faith, will bring you to a place where you lack nothing. Through this powerful force, God will fulfill His promises to you. Follow the example of those who through faith and patience inherit the promises.

Faith

> *But without faith it is impossible to please him: for he that cometh to God must believe that he is, and that he is a rewarder of them that diligently seek him.*
>
> Hebrews 11:6

> *So then faith cometh by hearing, and hearing by the word of God.*
>
> Romans 10:17

Faith plays an extremely vital role in your relationship with God. It is multifaceted. Faith in God gives you power to subdue, conquer, and have victory over the world, the flesh, and the devil. Your faith also functions as a shield that quenches all the fiery darts of the wicked one. Faith is the eye that sees the unseen and the ear that hears the unheard. Faith is the voice of boldness and conviction of unseen realities. Faith shouts the victory while the walls of opposition are still standing.

Faith calls things that are not, as though they were. Faith declares the end from the beginning. Faith believes with the heart and declares with the mouth the promises of God until they are living realities. Faith is an action based upon a belief that God is, has been, and always will be. Faith makes the impossible, possible! Faith is an adventure with God. You were created to live by faith. Anything less would be disappointing to God. Faith without works or corresponding action is dead and unproductive. Living by faith is living with a positive expectation of good things happening in your future, based on the promises of God.

Without faith, it is impossible to please God. God is not pleased when you fail to receive all that He has provided for you in Christ. God gave you a measure of faith when you believed the gospel. It is your responsibility to grow and increase the measure of faith you have. By doing so, you can receive more and more of what He preplanned and prepared for you. Your faith will grow and increase as you believe the Word of God, meditate on it, confess it, and act on it (do it, obey it, and practice it).

Faith is the union of confidence and assurance based on a conviction that God can't lie. This confidence and assurance have its foundation in God's integrity and trustworthiness. You can rest assured that God will watch over, perform, confirm, fulfill, and do what He said. If He spoke it, He will do it. If He said it, He will bring it to pass. Not one promise will fail to come to pass. It is impossible for God to lie or deceive us.

Your faith in God makes you a powerful person. Read the eleventh chapter of Hebrews and take note of all that was accomplished by men and women who trusted God. Through faith, God will work miracles in your life and bless you, heal you, forgive you, restore you, deliver you, and manifest all His covenant blessings and promises. Trust and obey God and He will bring to pass all that He has spoken or promised. Faith makes you a partner with God.

Faith will come to you as you hear and hear the Word of God. When faith comes into your heart, it must be mixed together (united, commingled) with the Word of God in order for you to profit and benefit from it. A great example of someone who mixed faith with the word of God is Abraham (Romans 4). God gave him a promise that his descendants would be like the stars in heaven in number. At the time, Abraham was childless, and his wife was barren. He mixed faith with the word of God and Isaac was born. He did four essential things;

1) He believed the promise God gave to him.
2) He did not become weak in faith by considering that he was 100 years old and impotent or that Sarah was 75 years old and barren. He did not consider the contradictory circumstances that made the promise look impossible.
3) He did not stagger at the promise of God through unbelief and doubt. He refused to doubt God.
4) He grew strong in faith by giving glory to God and by being fully persuaded that what God had promised, He was able to perform.

Giving glory to God is worshipping, praising, and thanking God before the promise comes to pass. Being fully persuaded means being absolutely sure, totally convinced, and without a doubt. Abraham was fully persuaded that God would keep His promise and not lie to him.

Follow the pattern of Abraham's faith and receive all that God has promised. The promises of God must be received by faith and embraced as a right now possession. Faith is the hand that receives from God. It is the vehicle that transports the unseen, invisible realities of God into the seen, natural world, in which we live. Everything received from God has to be received by faith. Even the gift of eternal life has to be received by faith. It is not automatically yours because you know it is available.

What Jesus accomplished will have little impact on your life if you don't mix faith with the Word of God. Just hearing or knowing what He did will not benefit you unless you know how to receive it as a right now possession. You have to believe you "got it," then you'll get it. Most people will not believe they "got it" until they see it. That is not faith at all. Real bible faith believes it receives without physical proof. Take possession of everything Jesus provided by faith; believe it, study and meditate on it, speak it, decree it, declare it, confess it, and act on it. Jesus paid the price for you to have it, and He will stand behind His word and make it good in your life.

Finally, make walking in love, exercising patience, and living by faith utmost priority. God will do great and mighty things in your life. Failure to walk in these godly virtues will stunt your growth, neutralize your power, and give Satan an advantage over you that he should not have. Possess your inheritance by faith.

> *Therefore I say unto you, What things soever ye desire, when ye pray, believe that ye receive them, and ye shall have them.*
>
> Mark 11:24

> *But let him ask in faith, nothing wavering. For he that wavereth is like a wave of the sea driven with the wind and tossed. For let not that man think that he shall receive any thing of the Lord.*
>
> James 1:6-7

> *And all things, whatsoever ye shall ask in prayer, believing, ye shall receive.*
>
> Matthew 21:22

You are an heir of God and a joint-heir with Jesus Christ. It is God's good pleasure to give you the kingdom.

CHAPTER 3

Acknowledging Every Good Thing

*That the communication of thy faith may become effectual by
the acknowledging of every good thing which is in you in Christ
Jesus.*

Philemon 6

*Let us hold fast the profession of our faith without wavering;
(for he is faithful that promised;)*

Hebrews 10:23

*. . . For unto us was the gospel preached, as well as unto them:
but the word preached did not profit them, not being mixed
with faith in them that heard it.*

Hebrews 4:2

What God did in and through Christ has to be taken
personally—as if done for you, exclusively. Boldly acknowledge
who Christ is and what He has done for you. Then, by faith,
receive every blessing and benefit that He has provided.** When
this is done, Jesus will reveal Himself to you. You will know Him as
a present day reality and not just as a historical figure.

One way of acknowledging that you have received by faith is
by giving glory to God. This is how Abraham stayed strong in
faith—and that is how you will stay strong in faith. Giving glory
to God is praising, worshipping, and thanking Him in advance for
what He has promised and being fully persuaded that He will keep
His Word. Praise, worship, and thanksgiving are expressions of
faith that delight the heart of God.

You should never let a day go by without receiving what He has freely given, and acknowledging or expressing your gratitude to God for what He has done for you. Most believers would do it if they knew what belonged to them. *The truths that follow must be believed, received, confessed, and claimed as a right now possession.* God will watch over His Word to perform it, and Jesus will confirm the Word with signs following.

Now, let's take a look at what Jesus has done for YOU and what YOU have as a result of it. Keep in mind that the cross of Jesus Christ was a place of divine exchange. *Everything that was bad about you passed to Jesus (He took it), and everything that is good and righteous about Jesus became yours.* That is why the preaching of the cross is the power of God. You are an heir of God and a joint-heir with Jesus Christ. It is God's good pleasure to give you the kingdom. You have an everlasting covenant with God through the blood of Jesus Christ. You have covenant rights that entitle you to the inheritance Jesus made available for you. Dare to believe and trust God to bring His promises to pass in your life. Acknowledge daily, every good thing that is yours through your relationship with Jesus Christ.

> *For the preaching of the cross is to them that perish foolishness; but unto us which are saved it is the power of God.*
>
> 1 Corinthians 1:18

You have been accepted into the royal family. If you had been the only person on the earth, Jesus still would have come and given Himself for you.

Nothing can separate you from the love of God, which is in Christ Jesus.

— ❧ —

CHAPTER 4

Jesus Loves You and Gave Himself For You

And walk in love, [esteeming and delighting in one another] as Christ loved us and gave Himself up for us, a slain offering and sacrifice to God [for you, so that it became] a sweet fragrance.
Ephesians 5:2 (AMP)

No one will ever love you more than Jesus loves you. He loves you unconditionally. *He didn't just say He loves you. He proved and demonstrated His love for you by all the things He did for you.* One of those things is willingly laying His life down and giving Himself as an offering and a sacrifice to God for you. Many make light of this fact and take His love for granted. They place little value or significance on what He did. However, without His unselfish act of love, one day you would stand before God to give an account and be judged for the sinful life you have lived. Jesus loved you enough to prevent this from happening to you. He willingly laid His life down for you—so you could stand before God spotless, clean, and as though you have never sinned.

There are many reasons why some fail to believe in and receive God's love, but it is available to them twenty-four hours a day. I've met people who don't believe God loves them. They think they are insignificant or are of little value to God. Nothing could be farther from the truth. I've also seen people who have tried to find real love in all the wrong places. Lasting love can only be found in a relationship with Jesus Christ. We were all created with a desire to be loved and appreciated, but only God can fill that aching void.

Don't fall for the subtle lies and traps of the devil that will deprive you of the one thing you need most in life; to know the love of God. The Lord Jesus will reveal His love to you if you open your heart and let Him love you.

The depth of His love for you can't be measured. He will not withhold any good thing from you. His desire is to bless you abundantly. You are the apple of His eye and more valuable to Him than all the treasures in this world. You have been accepted into the royal family. If you had been the only person on the earth, Jesus still would have come and given Himself for you. Nothing can separate you from the love of God, which is in Christ Jesus. God will never hate you. He hates sin, but He loves you. His love sees beyond your faults and failures. He has new mercy and grace for you every morning. All you have to do is receive from Him by faith. Trust and believe in the love that God has for you. Don't ever underestimate the power of God's love to redeem you, to restore you, and to bless you; beyond your ability to think or even imagine. His love can reach you no matter where you are. This love is in Christ Jesus.

Confession: Father, I thank you for loving me super abundantly. I believe and trust in the love you have for me. I give you glory and thanks that Jesus loves me and laid His life down for me. He gave Himself for me so that I could have fellowship with you and have everlasting life. I am grateful for this revelation and will remind myself often that you love me. You're working in my life at this present moment, and nothing can separate me from the love of Jesus Christ.

When you know you have right standing with God you will reign in life through the abundance of grace and the gift of righteousness.

CHAPTER 5

Jesus Became Sin For You

For he hath made him to be sin for us, who knew no sin; that we might be made the righteousness of God in him.

2 Corinthians 5:21

For if by one man's offence death reigned by one; much more they which receive abundance of grace and of the gift of righteousness shall reign in life by one, Jesus Christ.

Romans 5:17

We are made right with God by placing our faith in Jesus Christ. And this is true for everyone who believes, no matter who we are.

Romans 3:22 (NLT)

Jesus became sin for you so you could be made the righteousness of God. Righteousness is right standing with God—the ability to stand in the presence of God without a sense of guilt, inferiority, shame, or condemnation. Righteousness is a gift from God. Jesus became guilty of every sin you have or ever will commit so you could have right standing with God. This is fellowship with God at the highest level.

Right standing with God is a gift that you could not earn on your own merit or good works in a million years. At your very best, your righteousness is as filthy rags in the sight of God. Jesus knew you could never have fellowship with God based on your own goodness because God is holy. So, He took your place as a sinner and became sin for you. His standing with God was perfect because He never committed a sin. When you trusted Him as your Savior, you became heir to His righteousness. It is all by the grace of God.

The benefits of understanding righteousness from God's point of view are numerous. You have been made righteous in the eyes of God. He does not see you as a sinner. He sees you as His child. God wants you to receive this gift so you can reign in life. Many are not reigning in life because they are under the condemnation of the devil. When they approach God in prayer, they feel condemned, guilty, inferior, and unworthy. When a person is under condemnation, they will lack confidence that God will answer their prayer or help them.

Condemnation will render you faithless and will rob you of the opportunity to receive from God or fellowship with Him freely. This is why it was necessary for Jesus to become sin for you. Sin results in condemnation. Jesus bore your condemnation, by becoming sin for you, so you could receive the gift of righteousness. He has provided for you righteousness (right standing) with God that could never be based on your performance. Isn't that awesome! Satan can never legally condemn you before God and has lost his power to control you.

When you know you have right standing with God, you will reign in life through the abundance of grace and the gift of righteousness. Righteousness gives you the ability to have fellowship with God in prayer and power on earth to do the works of Christ. Ministering the love of God to others and destroying the works of the devil are the works of Christ. Take your rightful place as a child of God and begin to rule and reign as more than a conqueror through Jesus Christ your Lord.

Another beautiful picture of righteousness (right standing) with God is found in Zechariah 3. Joshua, the high priest, stood before the Lord in filthy clothes. The devil was standing next to him to resist (accuse) him. The Lord spoke to Joshua; I am going to give you a change of clothes. The Lord removed the filthy garments and clothed him in clean garments, representing righteousness. That is what the Lord did for you when Jesus became sin for you. He removed your filthy clothing and gave you a robe of righteousness that allows you to stand in His presence without guilt or condemnation. When you understand this, you will know that Satan has lost the power to reign over you or to accuse you before God. You are ready to reign in life through the abundance of grace and the gift of righteousness.

Confession: Father, I give you praise, glory, and thanks for allowing Jesus to become sin for me. I receive the abundance of grace and the gift of righteousness as a right now possession. I have been made righteous in your sight. This right standing with you is not given to me based on my good deeds, acts of righteousness, or my holiness. It is given to me solely based on my faith in your mercy and grace through the shed blood of Jesus Christ. I have inherited the same right standing with God that Jesus Christ now has. I am in Christ and Christ is in me.

God never intended for you to suffer with the things Jesus redeemed you from.

CHAPTER 6

——————— ✄ ———————

Jesus Suffered For You

*For Christ also hath once suffered for sins, the just for the
unjust, that he might bring us to God, being put to death in the
flesh, but quickened by the Spirit:*

1 Peter 3:18

*For even hereunto were ye called: because Christ also suffered
for us, leaving us an example, that ye should follow his steps:*

1 Peter 2:21

These Scriptures reveal that Jesus' suffering for you was two-fold.
He suffered one time as your substitute for sin, and He gave you an
example of how to suffer persecution and tribulation as a believer
who trusts in God. He is the only substitute God would accept as
atonement for your sin. Therefore, Jesus has done for you what no
one else could do.

Many misunderstand suffering and have thought that it's God's will
to suffer with sin, sickness, disease, and poverty. It is true that Jesus
said you would have tribulation, test, persecution, and trials in this
world. We are not exempt from them. However, God never intended
for you to suffer with the things Jesus redeemed you from. He does
not want you to suffer with sin, sickness, disease, or poverty. Jesus
redeemed you from these curses so you could have the blessing of
the Lord.

His suffering for your sins began when He humbled Himself and
laid aside His mighty power and glory to become a human being for
the suffering of death. His suffering ended when He shed His blood

and died on the cross in your place, as your substitute. Jesus suffered for you so that He could present you to the Father without spot, wrinkle, or blemish. He suffered the shame, pain, humiliation and the penalty that you would have suffered for your sinful condition.

Jesus intimately acquainted Himself with the human experience by facing the same test and temptations that you do.

> *For because He Himself [in His humanity] has suffered in being tempted (tested and tried), He is able [immediately] to run to the cry of (assist, relieve) those who are being tempted and tested and tried [and who therefore are being exposed to suffering].*
>
> Hebrews 2:18 (AMP)

> *For we do not have a High Priest Who is unable to understand and sympathize and have a shared feeling with our weaknesses and infirmities and liability to the assaults of temptation, but One Who has been tempted in every respect as we are, yet without sinning.*
>
> Hebrews 4:15 (AMP)

Jesus was enticed, tested, tried, and tempted with every temptation that anyone would ever face, yet He didn't sin. No other person has ever been tempted as severely as Jesus was tempted. He suffered, endured, and conquered every temptation and trial, so He could be compassionate, understanding, and helpful when you are faced with life's trials and tribulations. He knows and understands how you feel and what you are going through. For this reason, He is your faithful High Priest and stands ready to represent you and help you in your time of need.

He suffered being lied on, tempted, persecuted, threatened, abused, falsely accused, criticized, and humiliated to leave you an example of how to trust God in the difficult places of life. He endured the hard places of life by placing His life in the hands of His loving

Father and trusting Him for righteousness to prevail. You can do the same thing too. Follow the example of the King of Kings.

Confession: Father, I give you praise, glory, and thanks for loving me enough to allow Jesus to suffer as a substitute for my sins. Jesus, the righteous, innocent one, suffered for me, the unrighteous, guilty one, so that I could have and enjoy a wonderful relationship with you as my heavenly Father. Jesus has presented me to the Father without spot or wrinkle because He has cleansed me with His precious blood.

Don't ever accept poverty as the will of God for your life. It is not! God takes pleasure in your prosperity.

You could say, God is not pleased when you don't prosper.

Jesus Became Poor For You

For ye know the grace of our Lord Jesus Christ, that, though he was rich, yet for your sakes he became poor, that ye through his poverty might be rich.

2 Corinthians 8:9

And God is able to make all grace (every favor and earthly blessing) come to you in abundance, so that you may always and under all circumstances and whatever the need be self-sufficient [possessing enough to require no aid or support and furnished in abundance for every good work and charitable donation].

2 Corinthians 9:8 (AMP)

The blessing of the LORD, it maketh rich, and he addeth no sorrow with it.

Proverbs 10:22

The rich man's wealth is his strong city: the destruction of the poor is their poverty.

Proverbs 10:15

The belief that Jesus bore our sins on the cross is universally accepted by believers throughout the world. The Scriptures also reveal that when Jesus went to the cross, He carried our poverty with Him. Poverty has been defined as the condition of being destitute of riches and abundance; not having enough. He took your poverty so you could be made rich. Rich has been defined as having an abundant supply; more than enough. Jesus said that He came that you might have life and have it more abundantly (John 10:10). This is good news!

The abundance Jesus was speaking of is more than material blessings and money, even though they are included in the blessing of the Lord. The blessing of the Lord also includes an abundance of joy, favor with God and man, truth, mercy, peace, goodness, riches, honor, wisdom, strength, family blessing, excellent health, gainful employment, long life, and everything else you would ever need to do His will.

Our God is a God of abundance. There is no shortage, lack, or poverty in heaven. If poverty is the will of God, then there would be poverty in heaven. There is overwhelming evidence in the Scriptures that God is not opposed to you being blessed or rich. For example, Deuteronomy 8:18 reveals that it is God who gives you power to get wealth. Wealth in this context was defined by God as material blessings; possessing good houses to live in, having their silver and gold (money) multiplied, having an abundance of water for their crops and livestock, having an abundance of food (fruits and grains) to eat, and an abundance of mineral resources. The Lord described it as a land flowing with milk and honey. The blessing also came with a warning not to forget who the blessing came from.

It is not the will of God for you to barely get by and not have enough to be a blessing to your family and those He has called you to minister to and bless. Don't ever accept poverty as the will of God for your life. It is not! God takes pleasure in your prosperity. God is not pleased when you don't prosper. *Poverty is a curse and leads to tremendous suffering, depression, fear, stress, stinginess, idolatry, and a multitude of other ailments and sins. Poverty deprives people of the joy that comes from having plenty for themselves and plenty to bless others.* It is the will of God for you to prosper spiritually, physically, financially, materially, and in every area of your life. Jesus placed poverty in the same category as sin. He bore your poverty just like he bore your sin. He bore your poverty so you could have His abundant blessing in every area of your life.

Expect God to give you opportunities to be blessed, so you can be a blessing. The blessing of the Lord can come to you in at least three ways. They are:

- Divine Instructions—these are instructions given by the Lord, that when obeyed, bring supernatural increase. In Luke 5, Peter obeyed one instruction to let down his net, and he caught more fish than he had ever caught in his life.
- Divine Favor—this is when God gives you favor with a person(s) who has power, ability, and influence to help you. Joseph and Nehemiah are good examples of those who lived in the favor of God.
- Divine Appointments—these are meetings with others that have been arranged by God for the purpose of blessing you or using you as a blessing to others. A good example of this is Elijah and the widow at Zarephath. God orchestrated their appointment, and they were a blessing to each other during a time of famine and drought (1 Kings 17:9).

In summary, obey God and do His will. God will supply all your need according to His riches in glory by Christ Jesus. Serve God with joyfulness and gladness of heart for the abundance of all things. Receive His abundance and experience the richness of His grace.

Confession: Father, I give you glory, praise, and thanks that Jesus became poor for me, so I could be made rich (abundantly provided for). I claim by faith the blessing of the Lord and the abundance that is the will of God for my life. I seek first the kingdom of God and His righteousness, and everything I need is added to my life. I have been delivered from the curse of poverty. My God supplies all my need according to His riches in glory by Christ Jesus, not according to what is in my bank account.

Jesus loves you so much that He does not want you to live your life under the curse of sin, sickness, or poverty.

He bore the curse for you so you could have the blessing.

CHAPTER 8

⠿

Jesus Was Made A Curse For You

> *Christ hath redeemed us from the curse of the law, being made a curse for us: for it is written, Cursed is every one that hangeth on a tree: That the blessing of Abraham might come on the Gentiles through Jesus Christ; that we might receive the promise of the Spirit through faith.*
>
> Galatians 3:13-14

Here, we discover another wonderful truth of Jesus doing something on your behalf, for your benefit. Jesus was made a curse for you for two reasons: (1) that the blessing of Abraham would come upon you and (2) that you might receive the promise of the Holy Spirit by faith. Jesus took the curse of your disobedience and rebellion and in the process redeemed you from the curse of the law. The curse of the law includes premature death, sickness, disease, poverty, fear, depression, bondage to your enemies, spiritual weakness, mental anxiety, broken relationships, and a host of other conditions that are present in our world because of sin.

The word "redeem" means to buy back through the payment of a price. Jesus paid the price for your sins by shedding His blood on the cross and giving His life in exchange for yours. Jesus was cursed with your curse when He went to the cross. The curse of your disobedience came upon Jesus, and when you trusted in Jesus Christ as your Savior and Redeemer, the blessing of Abraham came upon you. The blessing of Abraham is the blessing of the Lord, and it is yours to enjoy.

This blessing is an empowerment by God to prosper spiritually, physically, financially, mentally, and in every area of your life through the power of the Holy Spirit. The blessing includes eternal life, deliverance from sin, power over the devil, peace, wisdom, love, joy, prosperity, good health, family blessing, victory over your enemies, and a host of other blessings that make life enjoyable. God has set before you life and death—blessing and cursing. He instructs you to choose life and to love Him with all your heart. You choose life when you choose Christ.

Jesus loves you so much that He does not want you to live your life under the curse of sin, sickness, or poverty. He bore the curse for you so that you could have the blessing. The Holy Spirit will teach and reveal to you all that Jesus has provided for you, so you can have fellowship with God at the highest level, do the will of God and have heaven on earth. Now acknowledge what He has done for you and by faith claim the blessing of Abraham and the promise of the Holy Spirit.

Confession: Father, I give you glory, praise, and thanks that I have been redeemed. Jesus was made a curse for me when He hung on the cross so the blessing of Abraham would come upon me. I claim this blessing as a right now possession. I also thank you for the Holy Spirit who leads and guides me into all truth and gives me power to live a life that is pleasing to you and a blessing to others. Thank you for boldness to share my faith with others who need your grace, mercy, and blessing.

Jesus unselfishly laid His life down, gave Himself on the cross, and suffered your punishment for sin so you could be joined to God and delivered from this present evil world.

CHAPTER 9

Jesus Laid His Life Down And Gave Himself For Your Sins

Who gave himself for our sins, that he might deliver us from this present evil world, according to the will of God and our Father:

Galatians 1:4

Who gave himself for us, that he might redeem us from all iniquity, and purify unto himself a peculiar people, zealous of good works.

Titus 2:14

Hereby perceive we the love of God, because he laid down his life for us: and we ought to lay down our lives for the brethren.
1 John 3:16

Therefore doth my Father love me, because I lay down my life, that I might take it again. No man taketh it from me, but I lay it down of myself. I have power to lay it down, and I have power to take it again. This commandment have I received of my Father.

John 10:17-18

Jesus willingly laid down His life and gave it in exchange for yours. His life was not taken from Him. He gave His life on the cross for you—to rescue you from the awful penalty of sin. I liken it to a guilty criminal standing before a judge. The criminal has just received a death sentence for the horrendous crimes he has committed. The penalty of death by execution for his crimes is just, fair, and deserving. However, an innocent stranger in the courtroom approaches the bench and begins a conversation with the judge. The stranger expresses his great love for the criminal and willingly offers to give his life and die in place of the criminal. The judge accepts his offer, over the objections of the prosecutor, and the stranger is carried off to be executed. The judge quickly turns his attention to the criminal and tells him "you are free to go; another has taken your place." The criminal is set free. His record is expunged, and he is overwhelmed with joy and relief.

In this illustration, Jesus is the stranger. You are the criminal. The prosecutor is the devil, and God is the judge. This is a simplified picture of what Jesus did for you when He gave His life for you. All you have to do is receive the gift of salvation and eternal life. You can trust in and place your life in the hands of someone who loves you so much that He would die for you. When you give your life to Jesus, He will give you a new heart and a new life. He will blot out the record of your past life, as though it never existed.

> *This means that anyone who belongs to Christ has become a new person. The old life is gone; a new life has begun!*
> 2 Corinthians 5:17 (NLT)

Jesus unselfishly laid His life down, gave Himself on the cross, and suffered your punishment for sin. He did this so you could be joined to God, delivered from this present evil world, redeemed from all iniquity, purified from sin, and be zealous and enthusiastic about doing good works (deeds that honor and glorify God). You are His ambassador to the world. You are in this world, but not of it. You will have to resist the temptation and pressure that the devil and the world will put upon you to conform. By faith, you can overcome anything (trouble, hardship, disappointment, etc.) the world brings against you. Greater is He who is in you than he who is in the world. The victory is yours.

The resurrection of Jesus Christ from the dead sealed the deal. He took up His life again when God raised Him from the dead. The same power that raised Jesus from the dead is in you. You have resurrection power in you through your union with Jesus Christ. How can you lose if you receive and walk in all that Jesus has provided. You were created to reign and win in life.

Confession: Father, I give you glory, praise, and thanks that Jesus gave Himself for me and now I am delivered from this evil world and the power of darkness. He laid His life down for me, and I am grateful. I have a new life in Christ. I am born again. I have been raised to a new life in Christ. I am in Christ and He is in me. I have been redeemed from all iniquity.

Jesus bore your sicknesses on the cross so you wouldn't have to bear them. Healing and restoration of health are covenant benefits and blessings you receive by faith.

CHAPTER 10

Jesus Bore Your Sicknesses And Diseases

Surely he hath borne our griefs, and carried our sorrows: yet we did esteem him stricken, smitten of God, and afflicted. But he was wounded for our transgressions, he was bruised for our iniquities: the chastisement of our peace was upon him; and with his stripes we are healed.

Isaiah 53:3-5

And thus He fulfilled what was spoken by the prophet Isaiah, He Himself took [in order to carry away] our weaknesses and infirmities and bore away our diseases. [Isa. 53:4.] . . .

Matthew 8:17 (AMP)

Who his own self bare our sins in his own body on the tree, that we, being dead to sins, should live unto righteousness: by whose stripes ye were healed.

1 Peter 2:24

God provided such a complete redemption and deliverance for us that it even included healing and divine health. Know that God does not punish people with sickness or disease to teach them a lesson. He is in the healing business, not the business of making people sick and destroying their lives. In the Bible, God The Father called sickness and disease a curse. Jesus called it bondage. The Holy Spirit identified it as oppression from the devil.

How God anointed Jesus of Nazareth with the Holy Ghost and with power: who went about doing good, and healing all that were oppressed of the devil; for God was with him.

Acts 10:38

It is not the will of God for you to be sick and diseased. It is His will that you be healthy and whole. So many are confused and struggle trying to discern the will of God in this area. If you want to know the will of God, all you have to do is look at Jesus. He is the image of the invisible God who came into the world to do God's will. Jesus never refused to heal anyone who came to Him for healing. He never told anyone that it was God's will for them to remain sick. Sickness and disease are a by-product of sin and has caused untold misery, pain, suffering, financial loss, and premature death. It is clearly a thief and an enemy of God. Let me explain:

First, there is no sickness or disease in heaven, so it can't be the will of God on earth.

Second, if God put a sickness or disease on someone, no one would be able to remove it and undo God's work.

Third, if being sick is the will of God, why do people go to the doctor or hospital to get well and get out of the will of God?

Fourth, God is our Creator, and He created the body with an immunization system to fight sickness and disease. We have a built-in healing system that is designed to keep us healthy.

Fifth, God has provided several ways you can receive His healing power; a) through the laying on of hands, b) gifts of healing, c) the prayer of faith prayed by the Elders of the church or other believers, d) miracles, e) casting out evil spirits that cause sickness or disease, f) a sovereign act of God, and g) God has given wisdom and knowledge to medical science and doctors who provide aid and assistance in restoring health through medicine and surgical procedures.

Further, we are instructed by the Scriptures to pray for one another to be healed. Peter, James, and John asked God to stretch out His hand to heal the sick and perform signs and wonders in the name of Jesus (Acts 4:29-30). Their prayers were answered, and many people were healed in the Book of Acts.

When Jesus went to the cross, He carried your sickness and disease with Him. Here, again we see the divine exchange that took place at the cross of Christ. God placed your sickness and disease upon Jesus so that you could receive His healing power, health, and physical wholeness. Jesus took the beating and whipping that you deserved, and it was for your physical healing. He was wounded, bruised, chastised, and shed His blood for your healing.

Jesus bore your sicknesses on the cross so that you wouldn't have to bear them. Healing and restoration of health are covenant benefits and blessings you receive by faith. Claim your healing by faith as a right now possession and give glory and thanks to God for allowing Jesus to suffer such a brutal, unmerciful beating, so you could be healed and walk in health. By His stripes, you are healed. (See 3 John 2, Psalm 103:2-4, Exodus 15:26, and James 5:14-16)

Confession: Father, I give you glory, praise, and thanks that Jesus bore my sickness and disease in His own body when He was on the cross so that I could be healed and walk in health. I receive as a right now possession your love and healing power, and I declare by faith that I am healed by His stripes. Thank you for this wonderful benefit of being in the family of God.

Jesus paid the price for you to have His joy and gladness at all times, regardless of your circumstances. The kingdom of God is a kingdom of joy and gladness. There are no sad people in heaven.

You don't have to wait to get to heaven to experience real joy. You can have fullness of joy now!

CHAPTER 11

❧

Jesus Carried Your Sorrows

He is despised and rejected of men; a man of sorrows, and acquainted with grief: and we hid as it were our faces from him; he was despised, and we esteemed him not. Surely he hath borne our griefs, and carried our sorrows: yet we did esteem him stricken, smitten of God, and afflicted.

Isaiah 53:3-4

And the ransomed of the LORD shall return, and come to Zion with songs and everlasting joy upon their heads: they shall obtain joy and gladness, and sorrow and sighing shall flee away.

Isaiah 35:10

Sorrow is defined here as deep mental or physical distress, despair, anguish, pain, sadness, toil, or hardship. It also means to be greatly troubled, in heaviness, or depressed. Sorrow is often caused by loss, injury, affliction, disappointment, or regret. Sorrow has been a part of the human experience since the fall of Adam in the Garden of Eden. Sorrow is a consequence of sin. If you willfully disobey God, you will eventually reap a harvest of sorrow. It is an unavoidable consequence of disobedience. After their fall from grace, God told Adam that he would till the ground for food, in sorrow. He told Eve that she would give birth to children, in sorrow. There are many unhappy people in our world who are breaking down under the heavy load of sorrow, grief, and sadness, but it is not the will of God.

Jesus did something about your sorrow when He went to the cross. When He was in the Garden of Gethsemane, just before

His crucifixion, He began to be extremely sorrowful and very heavy and said, "My soul is exceeding sorrowful, even unto death" (Matthew 26:38). The Amplified Bible translation says, "My soul is very sad and deeply grieved, so that I am almost dying of sorrow." The burden of sorrow was so heavy He almost died before He went to the cross. After a time of prayer, an angel from heaven came to Him and strengthened Him for the journey to the cross. Jesus was experiencing the sorrow caused by your sins. God placed your sorrow upon Jesus, and He carried it to the cross with Him so you could have rest for your soul, joy, and gladness. God does not want you to be burdened down with the cares of this life and live in depression. You should not go to bed sad, wake up sad, and have sadness all day long. Sorrow of heart causes many to have mental breakdowns, commit suicide, or make decisions that lead to years of regret and pain.

> *Come unto me, all ye that labour and are heavy laden, and I will give you rest. Take my yoke upon you, and learn of me; for I am meek and lowly in heart: and ye shall find rest unto your souls. For my yoke is easy, and my burden is light.*
>
> Matthew 11:28-30

Jesus paid the price for you to have His joy and gladness at all times, regardless of your circumstances. The kingdom of God is a kingdom of joy, rejoicing, and gladness. There are no sad people in heaven. You don't have to wait to get to heaven to experience real joy. You can have fullness of joy now. Jesus wants you to enjoy life, and love living. His joy is your strength and will carry you through difficult times and help you overcome the tests and trials of faith that are sure to come. Jesus was able to endure the pain and suffering of the cross because of the joy that was set before Him. He could look past His temporary pain and suffering and see the joy of salvation that would be a reality after His resurrection from the dead. Joy is the result of your faith, enabling you to see a favorable outcome beyond your current circumstances. In the middle of any test or trial, count it all joy, knowing that God will give you the victory through Jesus Christ.

The sorrow of the world and the joy of the Lord are not hard to recognize. When sorrow is present, there will be frowns, groans, moans, crying, tears, sighing, depression, and mental anxiety. When the joy of the Lord is present, there will be smiles, laughter, singing, rejoicing, dancing, shouts of victory, celebration, gladness, peace, and contentment of soul. Joy is a powerful spiritual force that will undo the work of sorrow and depression.

The joy of the Lord is maintained by fellowshipping with the Lord daily through prayer, study of God's word, and having healthy relationships with other brothers and sisters in the Lord. In the Lord's presence, there is fullness of joy. Guard your joy and don't let anyone or anything take it from you. Let nothing steal your joy. It is a part of your inheritance as a child of God. Ask God to fill you with His joy and by faith receive it as a right now possession. Sorrow and sighing will flee away.

Confession: Father, I praise and thank you that Jesus carried my sorrows so that I could have fullness of joy. I will not be overwhelmed by depression, sadness, grief, or the cares of this life. I will not break down mentally because of sorrow, regret, failure, or disappointment. I will count it all joy regardless of my circumstances. I will live joyfully and serve you with gladness for all that you have done for me. With joy, I will draw water out of the wells of salvation. Thank you for filling me with your joy. The joy of the Lord is my strength.

The peace of God serves as a built-in guidance system, confirming God's will and leading. Always follow the peace of God when you are making decisions about your future.

Trust the peace that God places in your heart and don't ignore it because it is a safe guide.

CHAPTER 12

Jesus Was Chastised For You

But he was wounded for our transgressions, he was bruised for our iniquities: the chastisement of our peace was upon him; and with his stripes we are healed.

Isaiah 53:5

Peace I leave with you; My [own] peace I now give and bequeath to you. Not as the world gives do I give to you. Do not let your hearts be troubled, neither let them be afraid. [Stop allowing yourselves to be agitated and disturbed; and do not permit yourselves to be fearful and intimidated and cowardly and unsettled.]

John 14:27 (AMP)

And through Christ, God has brought all things back to himself again—things on earth and things in heaven. God made peace through the blood of Christ's death on the cross.

Colossians 1:20 (NCV)

To chasten means to correct by inflicting suffering or punishment. There are several words used in Isaiah 53 to describe the brutal punishment that Jesus suffered for your sins. They are: afflicted, oppressed, pierced, crushed, stricken, smitten, wounded, stripes, and bruised. God chastened Jesus Christ in your place when He went to the cross. He took your whipping. Jesus was chastened so that you could have peace and well-being.

God withholds His peace from the wicked, but the righteous shall be led forth with peace. Peace is a blessing from the Lord. Having the peace of God in your heart provides multiple benefits for you. The peace of God serves as a built-in guidance system, confirming God's will and leading. Always follow the peace of God when you are making decisions about your future. Trust the peace that God places in your heart and don't ignore it, because it is a safe guide. The peace of God will save your life because it will keep you from being in the wrong place, at the wrong time, with the wrong people. Many have died prematurely because they couldn't recognize, ignored, or violated the peace of God. If you don't have peace about doing something, don't do it.

> *And let the peace (soul harmony which comes) from Christ rule (act as umpire continually) in your hearts [deciding and settling with finality all questions that arise in your minds, in that peaceful state] to which as [members of Christ's] one body you were also called [to live]. And be thankful (appreciative), [giving praise to God always].*
>
> Colossians 3:15 (AMP)

The peace of God also guards and builds a fortress of protection around your heart and mind that conquers and destroys anxiety, fear, and worry (Phil. 4:6-8). It will give you a calm, undisturbed, disposition when facing uncertain situations and trials of faith. We are taught by the scriptures to make, seek, follow, and pursue peace. God has called us to peace.

Our Father is the God of peace, and Jesus is the Prince of Peace. There are several ways you can receive the peace of God. You can receive it by faith, taking it as a right now possession (Mark 11:24). You can receive perfect peace by keeping your mind stayed on Jesus and trusting Him (Isaiah 26:3). Too many let their mind wander away from Jesus and become overwhelmed with anxiety, worry, and fear. You can receive peace by increasing your knowledge of Jesus Christ and what He has provided for you. Grace and peace will be multiplied to you through the knowledge of God and Jesus our Lord (2 Peter 1:2).

Don't settle for the counterfeit peace that the world will offer you. It will give you a false sense of security. It will lead to wrong people and places and cause you to make poor decisions. This is the kind of peace that Apostle Paul spoke of when he said men will say, "peace and safety," then sudden destruction will come upon them, and they shall not escape. This counterfeit peace is extremely dangerous because it keeps people from recognizing their need for Jesus Christ and causes people to believe in a false salvation.

Finally, the gospel of Jesus Christ is called the gospel of peace. God made peace with you through the shed blood of Jesus Christ when He sent Jesus to die on the cross for you. Are you at peace with Him? Let this be a defining moment in your life. Receive the love and peace of God into your heart. Jesus paid the price for you to have it. Believe and trust God's word. He will fill you with joy and peace.

> *The LORD will give strength unto his people; the LORD will bless his people with peace.*
>
> Psalm 29:11

Confession: Father, I give you praise, glory, and thanks for giving me your peace through Jesus Christ. Jesus was chastised so I could have perfect peace. I will let the peace of God rule my heart. I will trust the peace of God in all my decisions. I will seek and pursue peace in all my relationships. I receive the peace of God by faith. I will not allow myself to be agitated, disturbed, or fearful. I will not let my heart be troubled. I refuse to worry or be anxious about anything. My heart is established and firmly fixed; confidently trusting in the Lord. I will live courageously and will walk in the peace of God.

We have been ransomed from the grave and redeemed from death. The depth of God's love and wisdom to help and bless you must never be underestimated.

CHAPTER 13

Jesus Gave Himself As A Ransom For You

For there is one God, and one mediator between God and men, the man Christ Jesus; Who gave himself a ransom for all, to be testified in due time.

1 Timothy 2:5-6

I will ransom them from the power of the grave; I will redeem them from death: O death, I will be thy plagues; O grave, I will be thy destruction: repentance shall be hid from mine eyes.

Hosea 13:14

For even the Son of man came not to be ministered unto, but to minister, and to give his life a ransom for many.

Mark 10:45

Wherefore, as by one man sin entered into the world, and death by sin; and so death passed upon all men, for that all have sinned:

Romans 5:12

There is only one God, and He is holy. God hates sin, but He loves the sinner. Nevertheless, His righteous nature requires that sin be punished. The penalty for sin is death (separation from God). There is only one way to be saved from death and escape the wrath and judgment of God. It is through a personal relationship with Jesus Christ. There is only one mediator between God and men, the man, Christ Jesus. He is the Savior of the world. Jesus is the only person who has never committed a sin. Therefore, He is qualified to represent you. Jesus gave Himself as a ransom for you. He gave His life in exchange for yours. (See Rev. 5:9-12, 13:8)

A ransom is a payment demanded for the release of a prisoner or captive. Jesus gave Himself as a ransom to rescue you from captivity and the eternal consequences of sin. You have been set free (liberated). He willingly laid down His life, accepted your punishment, and paid the price for your sin. You have been ransomed from the grave and redeemed from death. You are free from sin to serve God in righteousness and truth. Sin has lost its dominion and power to control you. You will spend eternity in the presence of God, not in Hell. Hell is a place that has been prepared for the devil and his angels. It is also the eternal destination of those who have refused and rejected God's mercy and the grace of our Lord Jesus Christ.

Romans 3:23 says, "For all have sinned and come short of the glory of God." This Scripture levels the playing field. It places all of us, regardless of race, color, culture, national origin, financial status, educational achievement, or religious background in the same category. There is none righteous, no, not one. All have sinned against God. It doesn't matter where you are in the world—Asia, Africa, Europe, or the Americas; you will find that man is a sinner. When Adam disobeyed God, sin and death entered the spiritual DNA of the human race—resulting in separation from God. Man does not have the power to change his spiritual DNA and free himself from the curse and stronghold of sin. He needs a Savior, a Deliverer. There is no deliverance from sin without Jesus Christ. Ephesians 6:23 says, "For the wages of sin is death, but the gift of God is eternal life through Jesus Christ our Lord." We were all slaves and prisoners of sin until we received God's gift of eternal life. When you received Jesus Christ as your Savior, He changed your spiritual DNA.

> *Therefore if any person is [ingrafted] in Christ (the Messiah) he is a new creation (a new creature altogether); the old [previous moral and spiritual condition] has passed away. Behold, the fresh and new has come!*
>
> 2 Corinthians 5:17 (AMP)

Finally, count yourself as dead to sin, but alive unto God through Jesus Christ. Present your body to God as a living sacrifice and an instrument of righteousness. Don't allow yourself to be used as a puppet of the devil, but as a vessel of God. Deny yourself the pleasures of sin for a season and take up your cross and follow Jesus. Honor God by the way you live your life every day. Give glory and thanks to God that Jesus gave Himself as a ransom for your soul.

> *And when he had called the people unto him with his disciples also, he said unto them, Whosoever will come after me, let him deny himself, and take up his cross, and follow me. For whosoever will save his life shall lose it; but whosoever shall lose his life for my sake and the gospel's, the same shall save it. For what shall it profit a man, if he shall gain the whole world, and lose his own soul?*
>
> Mark 8:34-36

Confession: Father, I give you glory, praise, and thanks that Jesus gave His life as a ransom for me so that I could be free from the bondage of sin and death. I count myself dead to sin but alive to you through Jesus Christ. I am a vessel of righteousness, and I belong to you. I am a new creation in Christ. I have been ransomed from the power of the grave and redeemed from death.

Can you imagine that? Standing before God without a single blemish or fault because of what Jesus did for you.

This is a demonstration of the great kindness, love, and mercy of our Lord Jesus Christ.

Jesus Reconciled You To God

And, having made peace through the blood of his cross, by him to reconcile all things unto himself; by him, I say, whether they be things in earth, or things in heaven. And you, that were sometime alienated and enemies in your mind by wicked works, yet now hath he reconciled.

Colossians 1:20-21

For since our friendship with God was restored by the death of his Son while we were still his enemies, we will certainly be saved through the life of his Son. So now we can rejoice in our wonderful new relationship with God because our Lord Jesus Christ has made us friends of God.

Romans 5:10-11 (NLT)

As stated previously, sin resulted in separation, alienation, and broken fellowship with God. Jesus shed His blood, hung on the cross, and died to reconcile you to God. To reconcile means to restore to favor, friendship, or harmony. Jesus gave his life to end the separation between God and man. He restored the fellowship and removed the hostility caused by wicked works and a hostile attitude towards God. Because of what Jesus did for you, God no longer considers you an enemy, but a friend. God has cleansed you from all your sins, treating you as though they never occurred. This is almost too good to be true, but it is.

Jesus reconciled you to God through His death, in order to present you as holy, spotless, blameless, faultless, irreproachable, and without blemish. Can you imagine that? Being able to stand before

God without a single blemish or fault. This is a demonstration of the great kindness, love, and mercy of our Lord Jesus Christ. You can continue to live as an enemy of God by doing wicked works, or you can choose to be a friend of God by separating yourself from sin. Just decide not to participate when people want to do things that dishonor God.

> *Yet now he has reconciled you to himself through the death of Christ in his physical body. As a result, he has brought you into his own presence, and you are holy and blameless as you stand before him without a single fault.*
>
> *But you must continue to believe this truth and stand firmly in it. Don't drift away from the assurance you received when you heard the Good News. The Good News has been preached all over the world, and I, Paul, have been appointed as God's servant to proclaim it.*
>
> Colossians 1:22-23 (NLT)

Because you have been reconciled, you are now an Ambassador of Christ. God has appointed you to tell others what He has done for them through Jesus Christ. He has given you the ministry of reconciliation. Tell everyone the good news and fulfill your ministry!

> *But all things are from God, Who through Jesus Christ reconciled us to Himself [received us into favor, brought us into harmony with Himself] and gave to us the ministry of reconciliation [that by word and deed we might aim to bring others into harmony with Him].*
>
> *It was God [personally present] in Christ, reconciling and restoring the world to favor with Himself, not counting up and holding against [men] their trespasses [but cancelling them], and committing to us the message of reconciliation (of the*

restoration to favor). So we are Christ's ambassadors, God making His appeal as it were through us.

We [as Christ's personal representatives] beg you for His sake to lay hold of the divine favor [now offered you] and be reconciled to God.

2 Corinthians 5:18-20 (AMP)

By faith, take possession of the divine favor that has been made available to you. The favor of God will surround you like a shield. This is a part of your inheritance as a child of God.

Confession: Father, I give you praise, glory, and thanks for what Jesus has done for me. He shed His blood and died for me so that I could be reconciled and be your friend. He removed the hostility and made us friends. He made it possible for me to stand before You blameless and without fault. I thank you that I can come boldly to the throne of grace to fellowship with you and receive grace and mercy in the time of need. I am an Ambassador for Christ and have the favor of God upon my life. Thank you for giving me the opportunity to share the good news with others.

When you made Jesus Christ the Lord of your life, you became heir to the greatest, permanent covenant of blessing in all of creation.

The blood covenant of Jesus Christ is an everlasting covenant.

CHAPTER 15

Jesus Shed His Blood For You

The gospel of Jesus Christ hangs on four major hinges: the miraculous birth of Jesus Christ, the shed blood of Jesus Christ, the resurrection of Jesus Christ from the dead, and the promise of the Holy Spirit. If you take away or nullify any one of these, there is no gospel at all. This is a major, not a minor!

> *For this is my blood of the new testament, which is shed for many for the remission of sins.*
>
> Matthew 26:28

> *Neither by the blood of goats and calves, but by his own blood he entered in once into the holy place, having obtained eternal redemption for us. And almost all things are by the law purged with blood; and without shedding of blood is no remission.*
>
> Hebrews 9:12, 22

Jesus shed His blood for you so you could be forgiven and cleansed from your sins, and have peace and fellowship with God. Jesus obtained eternal, everlasting redemption (a permanent release and deliverance from sin) for you by allowing His blood to be shed as an offering for your sin. Without the shedding of blood, there is no remission of sins. The word remission carries the idea of being released from bondage or imprisonment and forgiveness or pardon of sin (letting them go as if they had never been committed). This is awesome! Through the shed blood of Jesus Christ, God will cleanse you from your sin, treating them as though they had never occurred. This makes fellowship with God possible right now. Jesus truly is the Lamb of God who took away the sin of the world. There are many benefits to understanding the significance of the blood of Jesus. The Bible says you are washed, justified, sanctified, cleansed, and made righteous by the blood of Jesus Christ. The blood of Jesus also cleanses your conscience from dead works (the result of a guilty conscience) so you can serve the living God. The blood of Jesus protects you from judgment, and the wrath of God to come to all those who have rejected His Son. It also protects you from satanic dominance and oppression and gives you power to overcome all the devil's attacks. Revelations 12:11 says, "And they overcame him [Satan] by the blood of the Lamb and by the word of their testimony . . . ." There's tremendous power in the blood of the Lamb.

The power of the blood of Jesus was clearly shown when God instructed Moses to have each Israelite family kill a spotless lamb (one without defects) and place its blood on the two posts and lintel of the door prior to the final judgment upon Pharaoh—the death of the firstborn son in every family. The destroyer passed over every household where the blood of the lamb had been applied. The blood provided a wall of protection; a covering, or boundary that could not be penetrated by death. The Scriptures reveal that Jesus Christ is our Passover Lamb who was sacrificed for us (1 Corinth. 5:7). His blood provides a wall of protection that can't be penetrated by the devil.

You can apply or plead the blood of Jesus over your life, your family, and everything you own by the word of your testimony. The word of your testimony is your declaration of who you are and what you have because of the shed blood of Jesus Christ. Plead the blood of Jesus every day.

Christ redeemed you from the curse of the law (Galatians 3:13). To redeem means to buy back through the payment of a price. Jesus paid the price for your salvation with His own blood. Salvation can't be purchased with money. If money could buy salvation, only the rich would be saved.

You must know (recognize) that you were redeemed (ransomed) from the useless (fruitless) way of living inherited by tradition from [your] forefathers, not with corruptible things [such as] silver and gold, But [you were purchased] with the precious blood of Christ (the Messiah), like that of a [sacrificial] lamb without blemish or spot.

1 Peter 1:18-19 (AMP)

Who[The Father] hath delivered[rescued] us from the power of darkness, and hath translated us into the kingdom of his dear Son: In whom we have redemption through his blood, even the forgiveness of sins:

Colossians 1:13-14

You are redeemed from all iniquity and a sinful lifestyle, so don't submit and yield to the base, beggarly elements of this world. The blood of Jesus was the purchase price of your freedom and redemption. God purchased you from the slave market of sin with the blood of Jesus. By shedding His blood, Jesus also consecrated for you a new and living way to enter the presence of God. By faith, you can enter the holiest by the blood of Jesus with confidence (Hebrews 10:29). When you made Jesus Christ the Lord of your life, you became heir to the greatest, permanent covenant of blessing in all of creation. The blood covenant of Jesus Christ is an everlasting covenant.

Now the God of peace, that brought again from the dead our Lord Jesus, that great shepherd of the sheep, through the blood of the everlasting covenant, Make you perfect in every good work to do his will, working in you that which is well-pleasing in his sight, through Jesus Christ; to whom be glory for ever and ever. Amen.

Hebrews 13:20-21

Confession: Father, I give you glory, praise, and thanks that Jesus shed His blood to redeem me from sin. My testimony is

that through the blood of Jesus Christ, I am washed, sanctified, justified, forgiven, made righteous, and cleansed from all my sin. I have an everlasting covenant with God through the blood of Jesus Christ. It is a covenant of life, blessing, and overcoming power. Everything I receive from my heavenly Father, I receive on the basis of the blood Jesus shed for me.

I plead and apply the blood of Jesus Christ over my life, family, home, job, finances, and everything I own. I am covered and protected by the blood of the Passover Lamb, Jesus Christ. I have victory and triumph over Satan and all his works through the blood of the Lamb. I receive the promises of the covenant by faith and exercise the authority of the covenant through the name of Jesus. I am growing in my understanding of my covenant rights and privileges through the word of God. The Holy Spirit is teaching me how to walk in the light of the covenant.

I belong to God and am a child of God and a member of the royal family. I am a king and a priest unto God; to Jesus Christ be glory and dominion forever and ever. Amen.

Jesus did not die upon the cross for Himself. He died for you that you might live together with Him in eternity.

CHAPTER 16

— ⟨∞⟩ —

Jesus Died For You

But God commendeth his love toward us, in that, while we were yet sinners, Christ died for us.

Romans 5:8

But we see Jesus, who was made a little lower than the angels for the suffering of death, crowned with glory and honour; that he by the grace of God should taste death for every man.

Hebrews 2:9

For God hath not appointed us to wrath, but to obtain salvation by our Lord Jesus Christ, Who died for us, that, whether we wake or sleep, we should live together with him.

1 Thessalonians 5:9-10

The Bible speaks of three kinds of death: physical death, spiritual death, and the second death. It is important to note that God created man a three part being. Man is a spirit, he has a soul (mind, will, and emotions), and he lives in a physical body (1 Thessalonians 5:23). *Physical death* is the separation of the spirit and soul of man from the body. *Spiritual death* is the separation and alienation of the spirit and soul of man from God. It is characterized by broken fellowship with the Lord and a sinful lifestyle. The *Second death* is eternal separation of the spirit and soul of man from God in a place called Hell. If you die without Christ, then you will experience the second death. There is no second death for a child of God.

When God created Adam, he was full of the life and light of God. God breathed into him the breath of life. However, Adam died spiritually in the Garden of Eden when he disobeyed God. He passed from life to death. Because of his disobedience, sin entered into the world bringing with it spiritual and physical death, sickness, disease, poverty, and every evil thing that is in this world (Romans 5:12). We inherited the sinful nature of Adam. Man is a sinner and is spiritually dead to God and must be "born again" spiritually. Consequently, all of us were spiritually dead until we received Christ as our Lord and Savior. When you received Christ, you received eternal life and passed from death to life; from darkness to light. Jesus is the only source of eternal life. Hallelujah!

How beautiful is the grace of God? It is beyond description. How awesome is the love of God? No one can measure its depth, height, length, or breadth. It passes all understanding. Jesus did not die upon the cross for Himself. He died for you that you might live together with Him in eternity. He came that you might have abundant life. Abundant life is the life and nature of God in all of its fullness. You were dead in trespasses and sins, but God, who is rich in mercy, has made you alive together with Christ (Eph. 2:1-4). He sent Jesus to suffer and die the death that you should have died. On the cross, He bore the curse of sin, sickness, poverty, condemnation, and judgment. On the cross, Jesus identified Himself with your sin, became your substitute, sacrificed His life for you, and died.

His (Jesus) death was different from any other death because His death atoned for your sins. Mohammad, Buddha, and all the other religious leaders were not without sin, and therefore, could not make atonement for your sins. Death by crucifixion was not a beautiful picture. It was pretty ugly. It was a terrible way to die and was reserved for the cruelest of criminals. Death was slow and painful and often resulted from exhaustion, suffocation, and loss of blood. In addition to the physical pain and suffering, Jesus suffered the spiritual and emotional pain and trauma of bearing your sins and becoming the object of God's wrath. God poured out His wrath and judgment upon Jesus so that it would not be poured out upon you.

In Mark 15:34, when Jesus began to experience the full weight and punishment for your sins, He cried out from the cross, "My God, My God, why hast thou forsaken me?" For the first time in His life, He became separated from His Father. The Father had to judge and punish His perfect Son and the Son had to experience rejection and judgment at the hands of His Father. When Jesus had taken the full weight and burden of your sin, sickness, poverty, and rebellion, He uttered His final words from the cross, "IT IS FINISHED," and He died. He had finished the work of the cross given to Him by His Father. The work of redemption was completed three days later, when God raised Him from the dead. Jesus is alive! Salvation is now available to everyone. The Father is completely satisfied that Jesus has met all the conditions of atonement for your sin. Jesus paid the price for you to be born again and have everlasting life.

Again, we see the divine exchange at the cross of Christ. He experienced your spiritual death, and you received His eternal life, ending your separation from God. Anyone who believes and puts their trust in Jesus has everlasting life now. You were reconciled to God and given a place of favor and fellowship with God through the death, burial, and resurrection of Jesus Christ. God has not appointed a day of wrath for you. He has appointed a day of salvation, a day when you would receive His awesome love and the gift of eternal life.

> *Verily, verily, I say unto you, He that heareth my word, and believeth on him that sent me, hath everlasting life, and shall not come into condemnation; but is passed from death unto life.*
> John 5:24

> *For the wages of sin is death; but the gift of God is eternal life through Jesus Christ our Lord.*
> Romans 6:23

> *He that believeth on the Son of God hath the witness in himself: he that believeth not God hath made him a liar; because he*

believeth not the record that God gave of his Son. And this is the record, that God hath given to us eternal life, and this life is in his Son. He that hath the Son hath life; and he that hath not the Son of God hath not life. These things have I written unto you that believe on the name of the Son of God; that ye may know that ye have eternal life, and that ye may believe on the name of the Son of God.

1 John 5:10-13

Confession: Father, I give you glory, praise, and thanks that Jesus Christ died for me so that I could live together with Him eternally. I thank you that I have His life in me now. I am born again and have passed from death to life. I am a citizen of heaven and of the household of God. It is no longer I that live, but Christ that lives in me. In Him, I live and move and have my being. I count myself dead to sin, but alive unto you through Jesus Christ my Lord. (Galatians 2:20 & Romans 6:1-6)

SELAH
Pause, Calmly Think About These Things

Now, let's recap and take a moment to reflect on what Jesus did for you when He went to the cross as your substitute.

- ✓ **Jesus Loves You & Gave Himself For You**
- ✓ **Jesus Became Sin For You**
- ✓ **Jesus Suffered For You**
- ✓ **Jesus Became Poor For You**
- ✓ **Jesus Was Made A Curse For You**
- ✓ **Jesus Bore Your Sickness & Disease**
- ✓ **Jesus Laid Down His Life & Gave Himself For Your Sins**
- ✓ **Jesus Carried Your Sorrows**
- ✓ **Jesus Was Chastised For You**
- ✓ **Jesus Gave Himself As A Ransom For You**
- ✓ **Jesus Reconciled You To God**
- ✓ **Jesus Shed His Blood For You**
- ✓ **Jesus Died For You**

The cross of Christ was a place of great suffering and apparent defeat. When Jesus died, Satan thought he had finally conquered God and won. Thank God that the cross did not end with the death of Christ. Resurrection came! There are benefits and blessings associated with each accomplishment. Give the Lord thanks and worship Him and receive by faith what He has given to you. Ask God to give you boldness to share His word and these awesome benefits of serving Him. Be ready to share your faith when the opportunity comes. He will open many doors for you to share His grace with others.

Take note of what the Holy Spirit is speaking to you now. Which of these accomplishments is speaking loudest to you at this moment? Take it to heart, pray over it, meditate on it, confess it, thank God for it, and share it with a friend or family member. Don't keep the blessing to yourself. The best way to keep the blessing is to give it away.

You have been raised to newness of life.
The same resurrection power that raised
Jesus from the dead is at work
in you now.

CHAPTER 17

Jesus Was Raised From The Dead For Your Justification

Now it was not written for his sake alone, that it was imputed to him; But for us also, to whom it shall be imputed, if we believe on him that raised up Jesus our Lord from the dead; Who was delivered for our offences, and was raised again for our justification.

Romans 4:23-25

As I mentioned earlier, the gospel of Jesus Christ hangs on four major hinges, and one of them is the resurrection of Jesus Christ from the dead. The Apostle Paul wrote that if Christ has not been raised from the dead, then our faith is in vain, and we are still in our sins and men most miserable (1 Corinthians 15).

The resurrection of Jesus Christ from the dead is a fact. After Jesus was raised from the dead, He appeared to over five hundred eye-witnesses. He appeared to His disciples over a period of forty days and talked to them about the kingdom of God. These men and women turned Jerusalem upside down with their testimony and the signs, wonders, and miracles that accompanied their preaching. Angels were present at the tomb after his resurrection and asked the women who were searching for His body, "why seek ye the living among the dead? He is not here, but is risen:" (Luke 24:5). We have the testimony of Apostle Paul; whose life was changed when He met Jesus on the road to Damascus (Acts 9). Before his encounter with Jesus, he was the greatest persecutor of the church and became one of its greatest advocates. There are millions of people who are alive today that have received Jesus Christ and experienced His resurrection power. In addition, we have the witness of the Holy Spirit, who convicts men of sin and reveals Christ to them. Finally, we have the personal testimony of Jesus Christ.

> *Jesus said to her, I am [Myself] the Resurrection and the Life. Whoever believes in (adheres to, trusts in, and relies on) Me, although he may die, yet he shall live;*
>
> John 11:25 (AMP)

> *I am he that liveth, and was dead; and, behold, I am alive for evermore, Amen; and have the keys of hell and of death.*
>
> Revelation 1:18

It is amazing that one of the reasons God raised Jesus from the dead was for your justification. Justification is not hard to understand. In simple terms being justified means "just-as-if-I'd" never sinned. Because Jesus paid the price for your sins, God justified you and cleansed you from all your sin. When you received Christ, God forgave you, expunged your record, and gave you a brand-new life. You are now able to have fellowship with God based on what Jesus did for you and not based on your good works.

Justification was made real to me on the day I received Christ as my Savior. I asked the Lord to forgive me for all the sins I had ever committed. Then He gave me a vision of a giant chalk board that had all my sins written on it. It was covered from top to bottom and side to side. There was no room to write another sin; sin was written on top of sin. Then I saw Him take a giant eraser and begin to erase the record of my sins and my past. From right to left, He cleaned the chalk board until they were all erased and gone. Then, He turned to me and said, "See; I have forgiven you for all your sins, every one of them; they are all gone."

When I saw that my record of sin had been erased, and that I had been justified, my heart changed. Suddenly, a desire came into my heart to live holy, and I whispered a prayer to the Lord. I said, "Lord, help me not to mess the board up again. Help me to keep it clean." My heart was filled with the desire to please God, and I didn't want to sin anymore.

When I caught this glimpse, I knew that God had given me new life and a new beginning. I came alive that day and started to live. Before that moment, I had only been going through the motions of life without purpose. Life begins at Christ! Thinking back, I know today that the giant eraser in the hand of Jesus represented the blood He shed for me. He gave me the vision of the chalk board because I was a college student who sat in classrooms every day looking at a chalk board (there were no personal computers in those days). It was easy for me to understand what He was communicating to me. He will reveal Himself to you in a way that you can understand and appreciate what He has done for you.

> *For by grace are ye saved through faith; and that not of yourselves: it is the gift of God: Not of works, lest any man should boast.*
>
> Ephesians 2:8-9

> *For we also were once thoughtless and senseless, obstinate and disobedient, deluded and misled; [we too were once] slaves to all sorts of cravings and pleasures, wasting our days in malice and jealousy and envy, hateful (hated, detestable) and hating one another. But when the goodness and loving-kindness of God our Savior to man [as man] appeared, He saved us, not because of any works of righteousness that we had done, but because of His own pity and mercy, by [the] cleansing [bath] of the new birth (regeneration) and renewing of the Holy Spirit, which He poured out [so] richly upon us through Jesus Christ our Savior.*
>
> Titus 3:3-6 (AMP)

Salvation is a gift from God based on His grace. From the moment you received Christ as your Savior, He expects you to learn His ways and follow His plan for your life. You have been raised to newness of life. The same resurrection power that raised Jesus from the dead is at work in you now. When God raised Jesus Christ from the dead, He demonstrated His mighty power over Satan, sin, and death. Jesus is King of Kings and Lord of Lords. He has all authority in heaven and earth. He has the keys of death and hell. Don't trust anyone else with your eternal security. Jesus is alive! (See Philippians 2:8-11 and Ephesians 1:15-23)

Confession: Father, I give you glory, praise, and thanks for raising Jesus Christ from the dead. Thank you for justifying me, forgiving me of my sins, and making me righteous in your sight. Because Jesus lives, I live. My life is in Christ. I have been raised up together with Christ and made to sit with Him in heavenly place at the right hand of the throne of God. I walk in newness of life. Jesus is my Lord and Savior. I will never bow my knee to another.

Don't let the devil bully you with his threats of destruction and death. He has been soundly defeated by Jesus Christ.

One reason Jesus came was to destroy the works of the devil.

CHAPTER 18

ⓧ

Jesus Delivered You From Sin & Satan

Forasmuch then as the children are partakers of flesh and blood, he also himself likewise took part of the same; that through death he might destroy him that had the power of death, that is, the devil;

Hebrews 2:14

If the Son therefore shall make you free, ye shall be free indeed.

John 8:36

Giving thanks unto the Father, which hath made us meet (qualified you) to be partakers of the inheritance of the saints in light: Who hath delivered us from the power of darkness, and hath translated us into the kingdom of his dear Son: In whom we have redemption (purchased our freedom) through his blood, even the forgiveness of sins:

Colossians 1:12-14

Jesus conquered Satan, sin, and death through His death, burial, and resurrection. His victory over your adversary was credited to your account. When you made Jesus the Lord of your life, He set you free from the power of darkness and the bondage of sin and spiritual death. This freedom is real. You have been granted life, blessing, the power to live righteously, and freedom to worship and serve the Almighty God.

When I gave my heart to Jesus and asked Him to be the Lord of my Life, He received me and changed by life. I immediately began to experience peace, joy, freedom, and the love of God. I was liberated from sinful habits that had me bound. I discovered that I had the power to say NO to temptations to sin.

The Holy Spirit's continued work in my life, through the word of God, has resulted in the following changes:

- My beliefs and values have been transformed by the word of God.
- My spiritual eyes and ears are open.
- Childhood superstitions and horoscopes do not influence my actions.
- Powerless religious traditions lost their grip on me.
- Love, power, and a sound mind have replaced fear.
- I have a heart to love and serve others.
- My mind is continually being renewed to the truth.

The changes are too numerous to mention here, but I assure you that when you follow Jesus, He will lead you to freedom. You are warned not to return and become entangled again with your former yokes of bondage.

Don't let the devil bully you with his threats of destruction and death. He has been soundly defeated by Jesus Christ. One reason Jesus came was to destroy the works of the devil. You need not fear the devil. The Bible instructs you to resist him, bind him, rebuke him, cast him out, stand against him, trample him under your feet, and give him no place in your life. He does not have the authority to do whatever he pleases in your life. You don't belong to him. You belong to God.

God has given you His armor and mighty weapons of warfare for demonstrating the defeat that Jesus dealt to him (Ephesians 6:10-18 & 2 Corinth. 10:3-5). Submit yourself to God, resist the devil, and he will run in terror from you. Resist him with the word of God, the blood and the name of Jesus, and the power of the Holy

Spirit. You are an Ambassador of Christ and a representative of the kingdom of God. You have been commissioned to tell others the good news and have been given the authority and power to do it in Jesus' name.

We are sure of this because Christ was raised from the dead, and he will never die again. Death no longer has any power over him. When he died, he died once to break the power of sin. But now that he lives, he lives for the glory of God. So you also should consider yourselves to be dead to the power of sin and alive to God through Christ Jesus.

Do not let sin control the way you live; do not give in to sinful desires. Do not let any part of your body become an instrument of evil to serve sin. Instead, give yourselves completely to God, for you were dead, but now you have new life. So use your whole body as an instrument to do what is right for the glory of God. Sin is no longer your master, for you no longer live under the requirements of the law. Instead, you live under the freedom of God's grace.

Romans 6:9-14 (NLT)

Submit yourselves therefore to God. Resist the devil, and he will flee from you.

James 4:7

And these signs shall follow them that believe; In my name shall they cast out devils; they shall speak with new tongues; They shall take up serpents; and if they drink any deadly thing, it shall not hurt them; they shall lay hands on the sick, and they shall recover.

Mark 16:17-18

Confession: Father, I give you glory, praise, and thanks that you have delivered me from the power of darkness, the bondage of sin and death, and have set me free. I have freedom to worship

and serve you without fear and the authority and power to resist and destroy the works of the devil. I am more than a conqueror, and greater is He that is in me than he who is in the world. I'm in Christ and Christ is in me!

The Holy Spirit will lead and guide you
into all truth, show you things to come,
and reveal to you the things that God
has freely given you.

CHAPTER 19

Jesus Sent The Holy Spirit To Give You Life And Power

Nevertheless I tell you the truth; It is expedient for you that I go away: for if I go not away, the Comforter will not come unto you; but if I depart, I will send him unto you.

John 16:7

But the Comforter, which is the Holy Ghost, whom the Father will send in my name, he shall teach you all things, and bring all things to your remembrance, whatsoever I have said unto you.

John 14:26

The gospel of Jesus Christ is not complete without the fulfillment of the promise of the Holy Spirit. Jesus called the Holy Spirit, the Spirit of Life, the Spirit of Truth, the Counselor, the Comforter, and the Spirit of the Lord. In Isaiah 11:2, the Holy Spirit is the spirit of wisdom and understanding, the spirit of counsel and might, and the spirit of knowledge and the fear of God. I like to say it this way. Jesus is God's gift to the world; the Holy Spirit is Jesus' gift to the body of Christ.

Jesus promised every believer that the same Holy Spirit that was present in His life would come to live in them. The Holy Spirit does the work of regeneration—changing you from a child of the devil into a child of God. When you received Christ as your Savior, the Holy Spirit imparted the life and nature of God into your heart and came to live in you. Jesus referred to this as being born again—born of the Spirit. Receiving salvation is like having a well of water in you, springing up into everlasting life (John 3:3; John 4:14). However, the work of the Holy Spirit does not end here. The Holy Spirit also does the work of empowering you to do the greater works of Jesus—anointing you to bring healing, deliverance and the message of salvation to others. This empowering is the result of receiving the baptism with the Holy Spirit. The baptism in the Holy Spirit is an anointing of power to live righteously, to preach and teach with power and demonstration, and to do the works of Jesus. Jesus described this as having rivers of living water flowing out of your belly—your innermost being or spirit (John 7:37-39).

Jesus was empowered by the Holy Spirit to fulfill His ministry and accomplish the will of God. Jesus healed the sick, raised the dead, and cast out devils because He was anointed by the Holy Spirit. The Holy Spirit anointed Him to teach and preach the gospel with power and demonstration. He was able to resist the temptations of the devil because of the presence of the Holy Spirit in His life. The Holy Spirit was always present in His life.

> *The Spirit of the Lord is upon me, because he hath anointed me to preach the gospel to the poor; he hath sent me to heal the brokenhearted, to preach deliverance to the captives, and recovering of sight to the blind, to set at liberty them that are bruised, To preach the acceptable year of the Lord.*
>
> Luke 4:18-19

> *How God anointed Jesus of Nazareth with the Holy Ghost and with power: who went about doing good, and healing all that were oppressed of the devil; for God was with him.*
>
> Acts 10:38

Jesus knew that for you to triumph over human weakness, overcome the world, live righteously, minister to others, and destroy the works of the devil; you would need supernatural power and strength. So he made provision for you by sending the Holy Spirit to be your companion and helper.

> *And, being assembled together with them, commanded them that they should not depart from Jerusalem, but wait for the promise of the Father, which, saith he, ye have heard of me. For John truly baptized with water; but ye shall be baptized with the Holy Ghost not many days hence. But ye shall receive power, after that the Holy Ghost is come upon you: and ye shall be witnesses unto me both in Jerusalem, and in all Judaea, and in Samaria, and unto the uttermost part of the earth.*
>
> Acts 1:4, 5, 8

Jesus instructed His disciples to wait in the city of Jerusalem until they were clothed with power from on high. He was speaking of the baptism in the Holy Spirit. When you are baptized with the Holy Spirit, you are able to speak in another language. On the day of Pentecost, Jesus baptized one hundred and twenty believers in the Holy Spirit, and they began to speak with other tongues (languages) as the Holy Spirit empowered them. Peter preached that the gift of the Holy Spirit, this baptism, was available to all believers in every generation (Acts 2:38-39).

Jesus Christ will also baptize you with the Holy Spirit—filling you with resurrection power, revelation, love, holy desire, and boldness to live for God. With this gift comes the ability to speak, to pray, and to sing in new tongues (languages). Ask Jesus to baptize you with the Holy Spirit and receive this precious gift and anointing of power by faith, by believing God's Word. The Holy Spirit will supply the words—words that are unknown to you—but understood by God, but you do the speaking. When you speak in an unknown tongue, you are speaking divine secrets, hidden truths, and mysteries to God. When you pray in tongues, you are praying the perfect will of God. Read 1 Corinthians 14 and Romans 8:26-28 to get a better understanding of these truths. In summary, receiving Jesus gets you ready for eternity. Receiving the baptism in the Holy Spirit empowers you to do the works of Jesus on earth.

When you received Christ, your body became the temple of the Holy Spirit. Jesus revealed many things about the Holy Spirit so you would know what to expect Him to do in your life. The Holy Spirit is the guarantee that God will fulfill all His promises to you.

> *In Him you also who have heard the Word of Truth, the glad tidings (Gospel) of your salvation, and have believed in and adhered to and relied on Him, were stamped with the seal of the long-promised Holy Spirit. That [Spirit] is the guarantee of our inheritance [the firstfruits, the pledge and foretaste, the down payment on our heritage], in anticipation of its full redemption and our acquiring [complete] possession of it—to the praise of His glory.*
>
> Ephesians 1:13-14 (AMP)

Without the Holy Spirit, you would not know the presence of God or have any understanding of what Jesus did for you. It is impossible for you to know God's plan for your life without the Holy Spirit. The Holy Spirit has been given to you to reveal Jesus Christ to you, and all that He accomplished for you through His death, burial, and resurrection.

> *Howbeit when he, the Spirit of truth, is come, he will guide you into all truth: for he shall not speak of himself; but whatsoever he shall hear, that shall he speak: and he will shew you things to come. He shall glorify me: for he shall receive of mine, and shall shew it unto you. All things that the Father hath are mine: therefore said I, that he shall take of mine, and shall shew it unto you.*
>
> John 16:13-15

Now we have received, not the spirit of the world, but the spirit which is of God; that we might know the things that are freely given to us of God.

1 Corinthians 2:12

The Holy Spirit will lead and guide you into all truth, show you things to come, and reveal to you the things that God has freely given to you. The Holy Spirit will speak to you, comfort you, encourage you, correct you, protect you, and warn you of danger. He will teach you how to walk in love, live by faith, stand in grace, and patiently endure until you receive all that God has for you. He will give you wisdom and power to say no to sin. He will strengthen you with His mighty power in your inner man (spirit) so Christ can live in your heart by faith. There is a sanctifying power that comes from the Holy Spirit that separates you from the world, and makes you an overcomer in life. The Holy Spirit makes you a partaker of the divine nature of God. He will create in you the fruit of the spirit which is love, joy, peace, patience, kindness, goodness, faithfulness, gentleness, and self-control. These are the character traits of Jesus Christ.

For we ourselves also were sometimes foolish, disobedient, deceived, serving divers lusts and pleasures, living in malice and envy, hateful, and hating one another. But after that the kindness and love of God our Saviour toward man appeared, Not by works of righteousness which we have done, but according to his mercy he saved us, by the washing of regeneration, and renewing of the Holy Ghost; Which he shed on us abundantly through Jesus Christ our Saviour;

Titus 3:3-6

The Holy Spirit will anoint and empower you to do the will of God. The Holy Spirit will give you supernatural ability to minister to others through the gifts of the Spirit (1 Corinth. 12). He will anoint and empower you to share your faith with others, destroy the works of the devil, and live your life in a way that represents, honors, and pleases God.

The Holy Spirit will always glorify Jesus. He will always direct you to love, honor, respect, appreciate, and obey Jesus Christ. The Bible warns us not to grieve, resist, quench, lie to, tempt, or blaspheme the Holy Spirit.

Confession: Father, I give you glory, praise, and thanks that Jesus sent the Holy Spirit to live in me, give me revelation of the kingdom of God, and empower me to do the will of God. The same Spirit that raised Jesus from the dead lives in me. As a child of God, I am led by the Spirit of the Lord in all the affairs of life. The Holy Spirit shows me things to come and is continually revealing to me the things God has freely given me. My body is the temple of the Holy Spirit.

Jesus is the Great Shepherd and Bishop of your soul, the great architect of God's plan for your life, who will never leave or forsake you.

He knows everything about you; even the hairs on your head are numbered.

CHAPTER 20

Jesus Is Representing You At The Throne Of God

For Christ is not entered into the holy places made with hands, which are the figures of the true; but into heaven itself, now to appear in the presence of God for us:

Hebrews 9:24

Seeing then that we have a great high priest, that is passed into the heavens, Jesus the Son of God, let us hold fast our profession. For we have not an high priest which cannot be touched with the feeling of our infirmities; but was in all points tempted like as we are, yet without sin.

Hebrews 4:14-15

Jesus has been raised from the dead and is seated at the right hand of God the Father. Few believers have an understanding of what Jesus is doing now at the right hand of God. *He is representing you before God and continuing to work on your behalf.* As your Advocate and Intercessor, He is defending you as an attorney against the accusations of the devil. He is interceding (pleading your case and praying) for you. He is acknowledging you before God the Father and the holy angels and has written your name in the Lamb's book of life.

Jesus is the Mediator of the new covenant that He secured for you by shedding His blood and giving His life. A mediator is one who stands between two parties, reconciling their differences and resolving their conflict. Jesus resolved the conflict that sin caused between you and God—giving you peace, favor, and fellowship with God. Jesus is the Author and Finisher of your faith and the High Priest of your confession. He is watching over your words and confession of faith to perform them and fulfill His promises to you.

Jesus is the Great Shepherd and Bishop of your soul. He is the great architect of God's plan for your life. He will never leave or forsake you. He knows everything about you; even the hairs on your head are numbered. He is carefully watching over you; leading, guiding and working in your life through the power of the Holy Spirit.

Jesus is the Head of the Church. He is building His church—directing its affairs and setting each member in the body as it pleases Him. You are a member of the body of Christ and should seek the fellowship of other believers in a local church. Do your part in building the kingdom of God. Let Him equip you for your assignment. Don't be deceived into not attending a local church. Don't isolate yourself from other believers. There are no lone rangers in God's kingdom. No one does the will of God alone. Jesus designed the church so that we would need each other and have to work together for the benefit of the kingdom of God.

In light of all that Jesus is doing for you right now, give glory and thanks to God the Father that Jesus is representing you before the throne of God, insuring that you receive your full inheritance of blessings, privileges, and benefits as a child of God. This includes a full measure of divine grace, opportunities, appointments, provision, and assistance to do the will of God. You will experience the presence and power of God.

> *For there is one God, and one mediator between God and men, the man Christ Jesus;*
>
> 1 Timothy 2:5

Confession: Father, I give you glory, praise, and thanks that Jesus is representing me at the throne of God. I can come boldly to the throne of grace by the blood of Jesus without a sense of fear, condemnation, or guilt and receive the mercy and grace I need to execute your will in the earth. I am grateful for your loving grace in granting me the privilege of fellowship, petition (prayer), and divine exchange.

I acknowledge that Jesus is highly exalted and has been given a name that is above every name. He has all authority in heaven and earth and possesses the keys of death and hell. He is the Head of the Church, The Author and Finisher of my faith, The Great Shepherd, The High Priest of my confession, and the Lamb of God slain before the foundation of the world. He is my Righteousness, my Advocate, my Healer, my Provider, my Lord and my Savior. I am in Him and He is in me.

SELAH
Pause, And Calmly Think On These Things

It's time to reflect again on the great grace that God has made available to you.

- ✓ Jesus Was Raised For Your Justification
- ✓ Jesus Delivered You From Sin and Satan
- ✓ Jesus Sent The Holy Spirit To Give You Life & Power
- ✓ Jesus Is Representing You At The Throne Of God

Your days of captivity and being a slave to sin are over. Jesus has resurrection power and desires to share it with you. If Satan had known that God was going to raise Jesus from the dead, he would not have inspired men to crucify Jesus. He played right into the hands and plan of God and suffered the ultimate defeat.

Jesus' victory over sin, death, the grave, and the devil was overwhelming, thorough, and complete. Satan is a defeated enemy. Death has lost its sting, and the grave has lost its victory. Jesus left no doubt that He is King of Kings and Lord of Lords. Jesus is alive, and God has raised you up with Him (Eph. 2:1-8). Because He lives, you have eternal life now. Take your place as a child of God and expect to overcome, conquer, triumph, and have victory in every area of your life. It is not the will of God for you to lose one, single, battle. You are more than a conqueror through Christ.

Jesus is alive! He is representing you at the right hand of God. He sent the Holy Spirit to help you represent Him and live a victorious life. Take a moment now and worship the Lord with praise, thanksgiving, and adoration that He is alive and living in you. Thank Him for His power working in you. You are a partaker of His divine nature. Greater is He that is in you than he that is in the world.

It is not the will of God for you to lose a battle. He has provided everything you need to have overwhelming victory. An overwhelming victory is a victory in which there is no question or doubt about who the winner is.

Jesus won an overwhelming victory for you over all your adversaries.

CHAPTER 21

Overcoming The Blessing Blockers

> *I beseech you therefore, brethren, by the mercies of God, that ye present your bodies a living sacrifice, holy, acceptable unto God, which is your reasonable service. And be not conformed to this world: but be ye transformed by the renewing of your mind, that ye may prove what is that good, and acceptable, and perfect, will of God.*
>
> Romans 12:1-2

In light of all that Jesus did for you, it is not automatic. You will have to overcome several blessing blockers designed to hinder you from receiving all that God has provided for you. They are:

- Ignorance
- Willful Disobedience
- Fear, Doubt, and Unbelief
- The Pride of Life
- The Lust of the Flesh
- The World
- The Devil

This is not an "all inclusive" list of blessing blockers, but achieving victory in these areas will propel you to victory over other hindrances that will arise. These can be overcome by the power of the Holy Spirit, pleading the blood of Jesus, utilizing the name of Jesus, and walking in the light of the Word of God.

Ignorance

Ignorance is simply having a lack of knowledge. Hosea 4:6 says, "My people are destroyed for lack of knowledge." The devil has a strategy to keep you ignorant of God's will and provision for your life. Refuse to be ignorant. Make the decision to let the Word of God be the final authority in your life. Read it, study it, meditate on it, confess it, live by it, and apply it to your life. These actions will cause you to grow and increase in the knowledge of God. Continue to renew your mind with the Word of God and His way of doing things. You will know the truth, and the truth will make you free.

Study to shew thyself approved unto God, a workman that needeth not to be ashamed, rightly dividing the word of truth.
2 Timothy 2:15

Willful Disobedience

Willful disobedience is refusing to obey or comply with an order or rule. This is what Adam did in the Garden of Eden. He made a decision to disobey God and committed the first sin. Adam chose death over life and the curse instead of the blessing. When you disobey God, you are also making the same choices that Adam made. When you obey God, you are choosing life and blessing. You can learn obedience by recognizing God as the supreme authority, submitting yourself to Him, and cultivating the fear of the Lord in your life. Another key to overcoming disobedience is cultivating the desire to please and honor the Lord in all that you do. Jesus did only those things that pleased His Father. His delight was in pleasing God at all times. Develop a relationship with God through prayer and bible study. Focus on doing God's will and pleasing God and not yourself. Practice obedience.

And he that sent me is with me: the Father hath not left me alone; for I do always those things that please him.
John 8:29

Fear, Doubt, & Unbelief

Fear, doubt, and unbelief are blessing blockers. Every believer will have to contend with this evil, unholy pack of thieves. They kept the children of Israel from possessing the promised land and caused them to wander in the wilderness for forty years. There are over 350 "fear not" scriptures in the Bible. God didn't give you a spirit of fear, but of power, love, and a sound mind. Perfect love cast out fear. Knowing and believing the love that God has for you will drive fear away from you. Don't be intimated and defeated by thoughts of fear. Fear is overcome by trusting in the love of God and knowing that He will never leave or forsake you.

> *Yea, though I walk through the valley of the shadow of death, I will fear no evil: for thou art with me; thy rod and thy staff they comfort me.*

Psalm 23:4

Doubt and unbelief will also prevent you from receiving God's blessings. Doubt calls into question God's integrity and results in wavering and unstable convictions regarding God's word. Another word for unbelief is unpersuadable. Believers are warned to guard and protect their heart from unbelief because it grieves the heart of God. Anyone who grieves the heart of God can't receive His blessings and will not enter the rest He has provided. The key to overcoming fear, doubt, and unbelief is studying and meditating on the promises of God until you are fully persuaded that God will perform and fulfill His Word to you. When you are absolutely sure and totally convinced that God will not lie to you, you will receive what He has promised and do what He has commanded.

> *He staggered not at the promise of God through unbelief; but was strong in faith, giving glory to God; And being fully persuaded that, what he had promised, he was able also to perform.*

Romans 4:20-21

The Pride of Life

Pride is the absence of humility and is characterized by self-reliance and living independently of God. Pride is a "chief" sin that opens the door to other sins. It is said, the proud seek not the Lord, neither is He in their thoughts. God resists the proud, but He gives grace to the humble. The only way to rid your heart of this demonic independence is through humility. Humility is one of the greatest character traits you can have. Humility acknowledges dependence on God, recognizes God's authority, and seeks, submits, and surrenders to God's will. Jesus Christ is our example in humility. God never rejects a humble heart. You can't receive from the Lord without humility and faith. Stay humble and daily acknowledge your dependence on God. Give God the glory for all the good things you achieve and receive in life.

> *I am the vine, ye are the branches: He that abideth in me, and I in him, the same bringeth forth much fruit: for without me ye can do nothing.*
>
> John 15:5

The Lust of the Flesh

The word lust simply means desire. "The flesh" refers to human nature apart from God. When we speak of the lust of the flesh, we are talking about sinful desires in your mind or body that lead you away from God—His will, plan, and purpose for your life. Your flesh is that part of you that does not want to do God's will. The fifth chapter of Galatians deals extensively with the lust of the flesh and how to overcome its weakness. If you learn how to be led by the Spirit of God, you will not fulfill (satisfy) the lust of the flesh. The Holy Spirit will give you strength to deny yourself the pleasures of sin for a season.

Another key to overcoming the lust of the flesh is recognizing the sources of sinful desires and thoughts. Eliminate those sources from your life. If you have a weakness for alcohol or drugs, don't hang out with those who drink or do drugs. If you have a weakness for gossip or gambling, don't fellowship with gossipers or go to the casino. If you have a problem with sexual lust, don't watch pornography or fellowship with fornicators. I think you get the picture. Stay away from people, places, or things that tempt you to sin. Avoid all appearances of evil. Count yourself as dead to sin, but alive unto God. Yield yourself (spirit, soul, and body) to the Lord and be a vessel of honor.

> *I am crucified with Christ: nevertheless I live; yet not I, but Christ liveth in me: and the life which I now live in the flesh I live by the faith of the Son of God, who loved me, and gave himself for me.*
>
> Galatians 2:20

The World

According to 2 Corinthians 4:4, Satan is the god of this world. The "world" refers to the age we live in with all its kingdoms and systems. He is the master mind and main influence behind the worldly kingdoms and systems that have been set up to remove the influence and knowledge of God from society. Satan is controlling the political, educational, financial, religious, entertainment, and social kingdoms of the world through people who are spiritually dead. These kingdoms are governed by the philosophy and mindset that man can create his own world without the presence, influence, or power of God. The devil tempted Jesus to worship him by offering Him the kingdoms of the world. Jesus resisted and overcame this temptation by guarding His affection for God, staying full of the Holy Spirit, and quoting the Word of God that was in His heart. Follow His example and you will overcome too.

Jesus said, "These things I have spoken unto you, that in me ye might have peace. In the world ye shall have tribulation: but be of good cheer; I have overcome the world" (John 16:33). He overcame the world for you. As a child of God, you are in this world, but not of it. Anyone who is a friend of the world is an enemy of God. You are not to conform to it or fall in love with it. Don't adapt yourself to, or pattern your life after those who don't have faith in God. You have escaped the pollutions of the world through the knowledge of God. Whoever is born of God overcomes the world. Victory over the world is achieved by your faith in God.

> Love not the world, neither the things that are in the world. If any man love the world, the love of the Father is not in him. For all that is in the world, the lust of the flesh, and the lust of the eyes, and the pride of life, is not of the Father, but is of the world. And the world passeth away, and the lust thereof: but he that doeth the will of God abideth for ever.
>
> 1 John 2:15-17

The Devil

Many don't believe there is a devil, but he is a real spiritual being. He is referred to in the Scriptures as: Satan, deceiver, father of lies, thief, wicked one, adversary, tempter, prince of this world, murderer, prince of the power of the air, destroyer, power of darkness, dragon, old serpent, and angel of light. From these descriptions, we can clearly see his character, and it's not good. He is full of darkness and lies about everything, every day. He can't be trusted. There is no truth or light in him at all. He is 100% wicked. Those under his influence and control carry out his desires and act just like him.

All of his evil plans and schemes to conquer God were shattered and broken beyond repair at the cross of Jesus Christ. Jesus destroyed the devil through His death, burial and resurrection. He stripped him of his authority to hold you as a slave to sin. He rendered him powerless to stop you from receiving your full inheritance of blessings in this life. He totally destroyed the works of the devil—sin, sickness, poverty, bondage, etc. Jesus has the keys of death and hell.

He has all authority in heaven and earth. Now anyone, anywhere in the world can be saved and delivered from the power of darkness.

Jesus delegated His authority to the church and commissioned us as His ambassadors to the world. This authority is released through His name. Jesus has given you the authority to use His name in prayer, doing good works, and in exercising authority over the devil. The devils are subject to you through His name. Jesus has a name that is highly exalted above all other names. You are to take dominion and exercise authority over the devil in your home, at work, and in your social circle. The key to exercising your God given authority is submission and obedience to God's word and will. When you submit yourself to God, you can use the name of Jesus and resist, rebuke, bind, cast out, stand against, overcome, and destroy the works of the devil. You overcome him by the blood of the Lamb (Jesus), and the word of your testimony. Don't be overcome by evil, but overcome evil with good.

> *Submit yourselves therefore to God. Resist the devil, and he will flee from you.*
>
> James 4:7

God Gives You Victory

In all these things, you are more than a conqueror through Jesus Christ. Victory in any area of your life is achieved by walking in humility (staying humble) and being submitted to God. It is not the will of God for you to lose a battle. He has provided everything you need to have overwhelming victory. An overwhelming victory is a victory in which there is no question or doubt about who the winner is. The loser is soundly defeated. Jesus won an overwhelming victory for you over all your adversaries. The blessing blockers have been soundly defeated. You can do all things through Christ, who strengthens you. Greater is He that is in you, than he who is in the world. Now thanks be to God who gives you the victory and always causes you to triumph through our Lord Jesus Christ.

Finally, make a quality decision to walk in love, serve others, and never hold a grudge or unforgiveness in your heart. Live by faith and trust in the Lord with all your heart. Submit yourself to God and refuse to yield to temptation. Instead of pursuing the pleasures of sin, pursue pleasing God and cultivate your heart to love, honor, appreciate, glorify, trust, and serve God. Put on the whole armor of God and commit to praying (talking) to God consistently. Position yourself to receive the plan and wisdom of God for your life by diligently seeking God. Then you will find your purpose, provision, and power for living. Obey the instructions given to you by the Holy Spirit—in accordance with the written word of God. Your greatest joys and opportunities to be blessed are ahead of you. The best is yet to come. The blessing of the Lord is upon you.

A word of exhortation: If you sin and get off track, you have an Advocate at the right hand of God, Jesus Christ. Be quick to repent and turn from sin. Confess your sin, forsake it (admit it, quit it, and forget it), and receive forgiveness and cleansing by the blood of Jesus. Then continue in fellowship with God.

> *If we confess our sins, he is faithful and just to forgive us our sins, and to cleanse us from all unrighteousness.*
>
> 1 John 1:9

Follow and obey the Lord for the rest of your life. When you do, God will bless you from this day forward.

When you look at all that Jesus has done for you, it is easy to see why He is the King of King and Lord of Lords.

He is worthy of your praise, worship, adoration, and devotion.

CHAPTER 22

Your Benefits Package

For ye are all the children of God by faith in Christ Jesus.

Galatians 3:26

The Spirit itself beareth witness with our spirit, that we are the children of God: And if children, then heirs; heirs of God, and joint-heirs with Christ; if so be that we suffer with him, that we may be also glorified together.

Romans 8:16-17

Bless the LORD, O my soul, and forget not all his benefits: Who forgiveth all thine iniquities; who healeth all thy diseases; Who redeemeth thy life from destruction; who crowneth thee with lovingkindness and tender mercies; Who satisfieth thy mouth with good things; so that thy youth is renewed like the eagle's.

Psalm 103:2-5

To open their eyes, and to turn them from darkness to light, and from the power of Satan unto God, that they may receive forgiveness of sins, and inheritance among them which are sanctified by faith that is in me.

Acts 26:18

As a child of God, you have an inheritance of blessings, benefits, and privileges that have been made available to you through the death, burial, and resurrection of Jesus Christ. You are an heir of God and a joint-heir with Jesus Christ. You are a member of the royal family of God (1 Peter 2:9). Your name has been written in the Lamb's book of life. Jesus wants you to receive your inheritance and enjoy it here and now. Now, let's take a look at your benefits package and put them all together to get a crystal clear image of your redemption and how much you are loved by God.

- ✓ **Jesus Loves You & Gave Himself For You**
- ✓ **Jesus Became Sin For You**
- ✓ **Jesus Suffered For You**
- ✓ **Jesus Became Poor For You**
- ✓ **Jesus Was Made A Curse For You**
- ✓ **Jesus Bore Your Sickness & Disease**
- ✓ **Jesus Laid His Life Down and Gave Himself For Your Sins**
- ✓ **Jesus Carried Your Sorrows**
- ✓ **Jesus Was Chastised For You**
- ✓ **Jesus Gave Himself As A Ransom For You**
- ✓ **Jesus Shed His Blood For You**
- ✓ **Jesus Died For You**
- ✓ **Jesus Was Raised From The Dead For Your Justification**
- ✓ **Jesus Delivered You From Sin And Satan**
- ✓ **Jesus Sent The Holy Spirit To You**
- ✓ **Jesus Is Representing You At The Throne Of God**

This is just a glimpse into what God has provided for you in Christ. The preaching of the cross is the power of God, because the cross was a place of divine exchange. At the cross, God laid on Jesus everything that was bad about you (your iniquities) so you could have all that is good about Him. Jesus willingly took your place as a sinner so you could be seated with Him in heavenly places (Ephesians 2:1-8).

- ➢ He took your sin so you could be forgiven and have His righteousness.
- ➢ He took your curse so you could have His blessing.
- ➢ He took your poverty so you could have His abundance.

- ➤ He took your sicknesses and disease so you could have His health and healing.
- ➤ He took your sorrow so you could have His joy.
- ➤ He took your chastisement so you could have His peace.
- ➤ He took your weakness so you could have His strength and power.
- ➤ He took your bondage to sin so you could have His liberty and freedom from sin.
- ➤ He took your alienation and separation from God so you could have fellowship with God.
- ➤ He experienced your death so you could have His life.
- ➤ He gave His life for you that you might live.
- ➤ He overcame the world, so you would not be overcome by the world.
- ➤ He conquered Satan so you could overcome him, resist him, rebuke him, bind him, stand against him, and cast him out.
- ➤ He conquered the grave to prepare a place for you in the Father's house.
- ➤ He shed His blood to give you an everlasting covenant with God.

Everything that was evil about you passed to Jesus when He was on the cross. Everything that was good about Jesus became available to you when you believe and put your trust in Him. Get a mental image of yourself standing before the cross and seeing your sin, sickness, poverty, sorrow, and all the effects of sin pass from you to Jesus. See Him taking your place as your substitute. Then see every spiritual blessing of life, health, and strength pass from Jesus to you. When Jesus shed His blood for you and died on the cross, He paid the price for you to have all these blessings and many more—every spiritual blessing in heavenly places. These blessings and benefits are for your enjoyment now and include:

- ➢ An everlasting covenant, eternal life, and freedom from condemnation.
- ➢ Salvation (deliverance from sin, bondage, corruption, and fear)
- ➢ Life, health/healing, & strength
- ➢ Fellowship with God and answered prayer
- ➢ The blessing of Abraham and prosperity
- ➢ The abundance of grace, mercy, and forgiveness
- ➢ The gift of righteousness & pleading the blood
- ➢ The promise of God's presence, peace, and joy
- ➢ The wisdom of God, guidance, and direction
- ➢ Victory over the world, the flesh, and the devil
- ➢ Divine favor, opportunities, and appointments
- ➢ Family blessing for a thousand generations
- ➢ Spiritual, material, and financial blessings
- ➢ The gift of the Holy Spirit
- ➢ Angelic assistance and protection
- ➢ The armor of God and use of the name of Jesus
- ➢ The fruit and gifts of the Spirit
- ➢ Long life and rest for your soul
- ➢ Access to the throne of grace

The list goes on and on. They are too numerous to mention all of them here. What a benefits package that is! Can you think of any other blessings or benefits that are not listed above? It is clear to see the depth of God's love for you. Jesus paid such a high price for your redemption. He has given you the Holy Spirit to reveal these great truths of redemption to you. Study, meditate, and confess them until you are rooted and grounded in them. Hide them in your heart and your faith and love will grow stronger as you experience heaven's blessings on earth. When you understand what Jesus has done for you, it is easy to see why He is the King of Kings and Lord of Lords. He is worthy of your praise, worship, adoration, and devotion. He is the only Potentate (Supreme Ruler). No one loves you more than He loves you. No one has or could do for you what He has done for you. He has blessed you for eternity with all of heaven's blessings. When you truly consider and appreciate all that He has given to you, you will be willing and eager to give something back to him.

Acknowledge, appreciate, and receive what God has done for you. Give glory, praise, and thanks to God the Father in the name of Jesus Christ. Acknowledge daily who Christ is, who you are in Him, and what He has done for you. Boldly receive the blessing and benefits that are yours because of your relationship with Jesus Christ. Claim, as a right now possession, these benefits of God's grace by faith (Mark 11:22-24). Every day you should receive from the table of redemption (blessing). The table of blessing has been set by the Lord. Receive what you need, enjoy it, worship the Lord for it, and then share the blessing with others who are sitting in darkness.

> *Whereby are given unto us exceeding great and precious promises: that by these ye might be partakers of the divine nature, having escaped the corruption that is in the world through lust.*
>
> 2 Peter 1:4

> *Giving thanks unto the Father, which hath made us meet to be partakers of the inheritance of the saints in light: Who hath delivered us from the power of darkness, and hath translated us into the kingdom of his dear Son: In whom we have redemption through his blood, even the forgiveness of sins:*
>
> Colossians 1:12-14

God made you a joint-heir with Christ. Everything He has, you are part-owner of it. This reveals how great His love is for you and how eager He is to bless you.

God Can't Say No

He that spared not his own Son, but delivered him up for us all, how shall he not with him also freely give us all things?

Romans 8:32

Since he did not spare even his own Son but gave him up for us all, won't he also give us everything else?

Romans 8:32 (NLT)

I call Romans 8:32, God's can't say NO scripture! This Scripture is straight forward and easy to understand. It says, since God gave Jesus for you, you can have everything He has. God made you a joint-heir with Christ. Everything He has, you are a part-owner of it. This reveals how great His love is for you and how eager He is to bless you. His love and grace are overwhelming and so full of wonder. Seeing all that Jesus did for you, what is it about you that would cause Him to do so much for you? He did it because He loves you. You are worth more to Him than all the riches and treasures of this world. You are important to Him and He wants you to have His best.

I in them, and thou in me, that they may be made perfect in one; and that the world may know that thou hast sent me, and hast loved them, as thou hast loved me.

John 17:23

Here's another marvelous truth that goes hand in hand with Romans 8:32. God loves you just as He loves Jesus. God does not love Jesus Christ more than He loves you. If He did, He would not have allowed Jesus to suffer and die on your behalf. He will not do something for Jesus and not do it for you. He has the same love for you that He has for Jesus Christ. That makes you pretty special in His eyes. Isn't that awesome! Think about this and let this truth sink into your heart. It is pretty amazing, but it is true.

When it comes to your covenant redemptive rights, privileges, benefits, and blessings, the answer is always YES. God loves you so much He would never deny you anything that Jesus gave His life to secure for you. All the promises are yes and Amen to the glory of God. The blood covenant of Jesus Christ is a revelation of what God willingly provided for you and proof that your redemption from sin is complete, and the blessings are yours. This is the reason you should have fearless confidence and boldness to ask and receive what He said is already yours.

> *And this is the confidence that we have in him, that, if we ask any thing according to his will, he heareth us: And if we know that he hear us, whatsoever we ask, we know that we have the petitions that we desired of him.*
>
> 1 John 5:14-15

All things in the covenant are yours, but you have to receive them by faith. The covenant is full of the promises of God. He doesn't want you to miss a single one of them. There is no limit to how much blessing you can have working in your life. Grace is unlimited. There are no limitations on the amount of faith you can have. Jesus never rebuked anyone for having too much faith, but He did rebuke those who allowed their faith to stay small and little. Little faith receives little from God, and great faith receives much from Him. Without faith, it is impossible to please Him.

Know and understand what Christ has provided for you and by faith take hold of what God has freely given you. By prayer and faith, receive the promises, benefits, and privileges as a right now possession. Then continually give God thanks, praise, and glory for them and wait patiently for them to manifest in your life. Believe and trust in God's love, power, and willingness to bless you with what He has promised. Live life to the fullest and then share the overflow with others. Remember, God can't say NO to you, and it is impossible for Him to lie. The answer is a joyful, generous, YES. May God richly bless you!

> *And all things, whatsoever ye shall ask in prayer, believing, ye shall receive.*
>
> Matthew 21:22

> *For whatsoever is born of God overcometh the world: and this is the victory that overcometh the world, even our faith.*
>
> 1 John 5:4

> *Let us therefore fear, lest, a promise being left us of entering into his rest, any of you should seem to come short of it. For unto us was the gospel preached, as well as unto them: but the word preached did not profit them, not being mixed with faith in them that heard it.*
>
> Hebrews 4:1-2

> *But let him ask in faith, nothing wavering. For he that wavereth is like a wave of the sea driven with the wind and tossed. For let not that man think that he shall receive any thing of the Lord.*
>
> James 1:6-7

> *Therefore I say unto you, What things soever ye desire, when ye pray, believe that ye receive them, and ye shall have them.*
>
> Mark 11:24

Jesus Christ is the only One who has truly made atonement for your sins and been raised from the dead.

He is Alive!

You can visit the graves of all the other false messiahs.

CHAPTER 24

Jesus Is The Only Way!

Satan has used religion to confuse and deceive many about the one true God and life after death. There are many false gods, religions, prophets, and teachers in the world. They often transform themselves into angels of light to turn people from the truth. They offer a way that seems right but results in death and eternal separation from God.

The Bible gives the world the truth. Jesus Christ is the only One who has truly made atonement for your sins and has been raised from the dead. He is ALIVE! You can visit the graves of all the other false messiahs. Many of them are graven images of man's imagination. They have hands, but they can't touch, eyes, but they can't see, ears, but they can't hear, and a mouth, but they can't speak. Don't be deceived by false religions that have established their own way of righteousness and have rejected God's way. There is only one door of salvation, not many. Jesus Christ is the door. There is only one mediator between God and men. His name is Jesus. There is only one plan of salvation and one Savior, not many. Jesus is the Savior of the world.

Jesus Christ was raised from the dead by the glory of God the Father. There is life after death with Jesus Christ. He is preparing a place for those who believe in Him and will return to gather His family to live eternally with Him. Jesus is coming again, and you need to be ready when He comes. You need to be prepared to meet Him if you should die before He returns. If you die in your sins, you will perish and suffer judgment and the second death. Please don't die without Him. Today is the day of salvation. Now is the accepted time to receive Christ. Let Him be the Lord of your life.

Let not your heart be troubled: ye believe in God, believe also in me. In my Father's house are many mansions: if it were not so, I would have told you. I go to prepare a place for you. And if I go and prepare a place for you, I will come again, and receive you unto myself; that where I am, there ye may be also. Jesus saith unto him, I am the way, the truth, and the life: no man cometh unto the Father, but by me.

John 14:1-3, 6

Neither is there salvation in any other: for there is none other name under heaven given among men, whereby we must be saved.
Acts 4:12

For the wages of sin is death; but the gift of God is eternal life through Jesus Christ our Lord.

Romans 6:23

That if thou shalt confess with thy mouth the Lord Jesus, and shalt believe in thine heart that God hath raised him from the dead, thou shalt be saved.

Romans 10:9

For ye are all the children of God by faith in Christ Jesus.
Galatians 3:26

And this is the record, that God hath given to us eternal life, and this life is in his Son. He that hath the Son hath life; and he that hath not the Son of God hath not life.

1 John 5:11-12

In this was manifested the love of God toward us, because that God sent his only begotten Son into the world, that we might live through him. Herein is love, not that we loved God, but that he loved us, and sent his Son to be the propitiation for our sins.

1 John 4:9-10

Prayer To Receive Christ

If you haven't made Jesus your Lord, ask Him to come into your life, and you will receive God's gift of eternal life now. Repent of your sins, believe in Jesus Christ with all your heart, and pray this prayer from your heart.

Lord Jesus, I come to you as a sinner needing a Savior. Please forgive me and cleanse me of all my sins. I repent and turn from my sins. I desire to serve you for the rest of my life. I believe you died for my sins. I believe with all my heart that God raised you from the dead. You are alive. I open my heart to you and invite you into my life. I receive you as my Lord and Savior. Fill me with the power of the Holy Spirit. Thank you for receiving me and saving me now. I am now a child of God and have eternal life. Jesus, you are my Lord.

> But as many as received him, to them gave he power to become the sons of God, even to them that believe on his name:
>
> John 1:12

Prayer To Receive The Baptism In The Holy Spirit

Jesus Christ is your Lord and Savior, and you have received the gift of eternal life. You have passed from death to life and have been delivered from the power of darkness. You are a child of God, and your name is written in the Book of Life. Hallelujah!

Jesus Christ is also the one who baptizes with the Holy Spirit. Jesus told His disciples that they would be endued (clothed) with power from on high when they received the promise of the Father—the

Holy Spirit (Luke 24:49, John 14:26). It is His will for you to receive the baptism with the Holy Spirit. The baptism with the Holy Spirit is also described in the scriptures as receiving the gift of the Holy Spirit or being filled with the Spirit. The baptism with the Holy Spirit is an anointing of power and is accompanied by the divine utterance of speaking in other tongues (languages). Jesus has not removed the gift of the Holy Spirit from the church, and this baptism is included in your inheritance of blessings. Read Chapter 19 again and the scriptures below and then pray this prayer to receive the baptism with the Holy Spirit. (See also Matthew 3:11, Luke 3:16, Luke 11:13, John 1:29–33, Acts 2:38, and Acts 10:38–45)

> *And he [John] preached, saying, After me comes He Who is stronger (more powerful and more valiant) than I, the strap of Whose sandals I am not worthy or fit to stoop down and unloose. I have baptized you with water, but He [Jesus] will baptize you with the Holy Spirit.*
>
> Mark 1:7–8 (AMP)

> *For John baptized with water, but not many days from now you shall be baptized with (placed in, introduced into) the Holy Spirit .... But you shall receive power (ability, efficiency, and might) when the Holy Spirit has come upon you, and you shall be My witnesses in Jerusalem and all Judea and Samaria and to the ends (the very bounds) of the earth.*
>
> Acts 1:5, 8 (AMP)

> *And when the day of Pentecost had fully come, they were all assembled together in one place, When suddenly there came a sound from heaven like the rushing of a violent tempest blast, and it filled the whole house in which they were sitting. And there appeared to them tongues resembling fire, which were separated and distributed and which settled on each one of them. And they were all filled (diffused throughout their souls) with the Holy Spirit and began to speak in other (different,*

foreign) languages (tongues), as the Spirit kept giving them clear
and loud expression [in each tongue in appropriate words].

Acts 2:1–4 (AMP)

Heavenly Father, your Word says that Jesus Christ is the one
who baptizes with the Holy Spirit, and that you would give the
Holy Spirit to anyone who asks. I am asking for this precious
gift. I want to be baptized with (filled with) the Holy Spirit with
the evidence of power and speaking in other tongues. Lord Jesus,
baptize me with the Holy Spirit. I believe I receive the baptism
in the Holy Spirit by faith and fully expect to speak in other
tongues as the Holy Spirit gives me utterance. Holy Spirit come
upon me and fill me with your presence. Give me utterance now
as I release my faith and begin to speak in new tongues and praise
and magnify God. Thank you in Jesus' name. Amen!

In the first moments after receiving Jesus Christ and the baptism with
the Holy Spirit, it is important that you tell a close friend or family
member that will celebrate your decision to become a Christian.

Read your Bible, pray, and continually seek God's plan and purpose
for your life. He has a lot He wants to reveal to you about your
purpose and destiny.

It is equally important that you ask God to lead you to a local church
where the uncompromising word of God is taught and practiced.
Join a church that will share your enthusiasm for Christ and help
you grow stronger in the Lord. Demonstrate true repentance and
your decision to follow Christ. Make a public profession of your
faith and be baptized in water.

Finally, purpose in your heart to follow Jesus with all your heart
for the rest of your life. You have just made the most important
decision of your life. God will bless you from this day forward.

May God richly bless you!

Contact Information

Greg Texada
P. O. Box 13195
Alexandria, LA 71315
(318) 442-8100

Other Books By Greg Texada

Christmas – More Than A Good Story

Praying Colossians 1